THE PEOPLE'S BOAT

THE PEOPLE'S BOAT

HMCS *Oriole*: Ship of a Thousand Dreams

Shirley Hewett

Heritage House

National Library of Canada Cataloguing in Publication Data

Hewett, Shirley
    The people's boat

Includes index
    ISBN 1-894384-20-2

1. Canada. Canadian Armed Forces. HMCS Oriole—History.
2. Training-ships—Canada.
I. Title

VA400.5.O74H49   2001   359.3'22'0971   C2001-910496-0

First edition 2002

Heritage House acknowledges the financial support for our publishing program from the Government of Canada through the Book Publishing Industry Development Program (BPIDP), the Canada Council for the Arts, and the British Columbia Arts Council.

Cover and book design by Darlene Nickull

HERITAGE HOUSE PUBLISHING COMPANY LTD.
Unit #108 - 17665 66 A Ave., Surrey, B.C. V3S 2A7

Printed in Canada

CONTENTS

ACKNOWLEDGEMENTS

*T*his is a love story. Its characters live in many Canadian and New England cities, their homes spanning five time zones. But affection and reverence for one of North America's most noble ships unite these kindred spirits who willingly shared their *Oriole* stories, photos, family archives, and dreams with me.

Sometimes, I think this book should be subtitled "The Story of Ten Thousand Conversations." Through my affiliations with the Canadian Forces Sailing Association and other organizations, I have been absorbing it by osmosis for most of my adult life. Since I returned from sailing in *Oriole* in New Zealand four years ago, I have pulled together threads from more than 100 people, by phone, fax, and e-mail. Victoria friends and clubmates—and strangers who quickly assumed kindred-spirit status—reminisced over multiple and varied potions and libations.

Many relatives and friends in the regular and reserve navies and in the University Naval Training Division have enriched my life and fuelled my passion for maritime history. As a child, I was entranced when the "elders" in my huge extended seafaring family spun yarns about our collective mythology: rumrunners and privateers, shipwrecks, shipboard smallpox, and storms survived. And how Joshua Slocum invited a close relative in Yarmouth, Nova Scotia, to sail with him on his last, ill-fated voyage. I have been privileged to spend the Swiftsure Race weekend on board various naval vessels: the Swiftsure mark and SAR ships, HMCS *Miramichi*, *Moresby*, and the CNAV *Porte de la Reine*. As a result, I learned about the teamwork that is an integral part of naval processes and deployments. Similarly, I did not toil in isolation when I generated *The People's Boat*. Without the loyalty, trust, input, and continuous support from my *Oriole* "team," you would not be reading these words.

I owe a huge debt to the good will and cooperation of the Maritime Forces Pacific, Navy Public Affairs in Ottawa and in Esquimalt—especially Lieutenant (N) Gerry Pash, Lieutenant (N) Andria Ink, and Sara Helmeczi—CFB Esquimalt Naval and Military Museum Administrative Assistant Clare Sugrue, and previous commanding officers and crew of HMCS *Oriole*. Lieutenant-Commander Michael Brooks had intended to write the ship's history to celebrate her 75th birthday in 1996. When we got back from New Zealand, he donated three cartons of invaluable documents that fast-tracked the research process exponentially. Lieutenant-Commander Larry Trim obtained other vital archival materials from Ottawa and Victoria. Lieutenant-Commander Scott Crawshaw welcomed me on board for many day sails and two outstanding short cruises, and patiently fielded multiple fact checks. Three years of continuous callbacks never fazed our longtime family friend, Lieutenant-Commander James Butterfield.

I owe another huge debt to the good will of the Gooderham family and Toronto's Royal Canadian Yacht Club. My hostesses in Ontario, JoAnne Gooderham and Enid Maclachlan, and Tawny Maclachlan Capon, Eve Pangman, and Royal Canadian Yacht Club archivist Margaret Brennan not only organized research for me, but also provided the gracious hospitality that gave me a visceral sense of the Gooderham family solidarity and *Oriole*'s origins.

From my professional world, I'd like to thank: *Monday* magazine editors James McKinnon and Ross Crockford, who taught me how to make every word count; my editor, Vivian Sinclair, whose expertise drove the final revisions that helped me fine-tune the manuscript; my publisher, Rodger Touchie, whose patience and flexibility accommodated the "head winds" that resulted when the volume and the complexity of the research caused multiple delays; George Cuthbertson, Paul Gartside, and Scott Rohrer for their technical input; my Periodical Writers Association of Canada (PWAC) colleagues Rosemary Neering, for her editorial input, and Bill Johnstone, for his ace troubleshooting that liberated me to go on the Odyssey 2002 cruise; and Renee Smith Valade (Canadian Airlines), who assisted with air travel to New Zealand.

Last but not least, thanks to my Caddy Bay "pit crew," who bought me time to roam. Patrick Finn, Mark Salter, Catriona Richardson, Anita Singh, Carmen de Mol, Kari, Ozard and Marshus Hewett, Crownover Steel, Carol and John Simson, Andrew, Suzanne and Ginny MacLeod, and Phyllis and Gordon Halsey kept the home fires burning, the garden watered, and the moggies appeased while I chased Kodak moments in many ports.

Thanks a bundle.

Shirley Hewett
Victoria, B.C.

FOREWORD

After Shirley Hewett dubbed HMCS *Oriole* "the people's boat," she could not help but portray its grand history through the many people who have touched and been touched by this vessel.

From the original *Oriole* through to the current and most durable *Oriole IV*, from its actual construction for George Horace Gooderham of Ontario through to its surprising success in the 2000 Vic-Maui Race, the trademark name is attached to more than 100 years of nautical history in Canada.

As the Canadian navy's sail-training vessel for junior officers and other armed forces personnel, a community public-relations ship, and an international good-will ambassador, HMCS *Oriole* has won the hearts of the military and the general public. At her Esquimalt base and in her adopted hometown of Victoria, British Columbia, she has been a common sight and integral part of the community for almost 50 years.

This book is published as *Oriole* prepares to defend five Vic-Maui trophies that came with the new millennium. They include the Royal Vancouver Yacht Club Trophy for "First Overall–Corrected Time," an award cherished by all Pacific sailors. *Oriole*'s grand racing tradition off the Victoria waterfront dates back to the 1955 Swiftsure—a venerable career in a time when new computer-generated hull designs and space-age materials and technology make modern racing yachts obsolete overnight.

The West Coast waters in which *Oriole* has sailed for so many years represent her fourth nautical arena. The first two *Oriole*s established a racing legacy for the "bird boats" in the last quarter of the nineteenth century. *Oriole IV* cemented this legacy in locations as diverse as the Great Lakes and Australia's eastern coast.

She spent her youth as the pride of George Horace Gooderham and family. His daughter, Mary, christened the vessel at her New England launching. Then *Oriole IV* cruised to her Great Lakes home on the Toronto waterfront, where she served as flagship for Royal Canadian Yacht Club Commodore George Horace Gooderham.

Later, while stationed in Halifax, *Oriole* raced in the waters off Lunenburg, Nova Scotia, home port of the famed *Bluenose,* and in the great harbours of Massachusetts, like Gloucester and Manchester.

The Massachusetts Institute of Technology still houses the original plans for *Oriole IV*. Shirley Hewett discovered them there and received permission to print marine architect George Owen's original drawings in this volume. Leaving no stone unturned, Shirley also travelled to Toronto to interview members of the Gooderham family, conduct research in the RCYC Archives, and peruse the logbooks that document *Oriole*'s Lake Ontario roots.

No ship can be divorced from its captain, and HMCS *Oriole* has enjoyed a long history of able seamen at her helm. From the hardy crew that steered her through the ice-filled waters of the St. Lawrence River when she was first attached to the Canadian navy through to her current command, "the people's boat" has been in good hands.

While Shirley's narrative uses first-hand interviews with many of the *Oriole*'s retired captains and kindly reminiscences to show the heart of her favourite ship, she has also searched far and wide to document the visual heritage of the *Oriole*. Her access to navy archival records and the personal photo collections of many of these retired sailors helps create a mosaic of memories recalling life aboard *Oriole*. And in describing her own adventures on board the *Oriole*, she provides us with a deeper look at the ship and the people who discover the sea through the opportunity to train as crew members.

It is obvious from Shirley Hewett's writings and many years of research that HMCS *Oriole* holds a special place in her heart. She disguises neither her subjectivity nor her belief that this good ship and those who define her heritage have earned her tribute. When all is said and done, *The People's Boat, HMCS* Oriole: *Ship of a Thousand Dreams* leaves us wanting to ensure that the great "bird sail" that distinguishes *Oriole* in any regatta will be capturing wind for another 50 years.

Rodger Touchie
Publisher

Sail-Training Ketch HMCS *Oriole*

Rig: Marconi-rigged ketch

Length overall: 102 feet (31.1 m)

Length on deck: 91 feet (27.7 m)

Waterline length: 63 feet (19.2 m)

Beam: 19 feet (5.8 m)

Draft: 10 feet (3 m)

Displacement: 92 tons (93.5 metric tons)

Mainmast height: 104 feet (31.7 m)

Mizzenmast height: 70 feet (21.3 m)

Freeboard forward: 6 feet 8 inches (2 m)

Freeboard aft: 4 feet 9 inches (1.5 m)

Total sail area: 15,700 square feet (1,458 m^2)

Working sails: 6,133 square feet (570 m^2)

Spinnaker: 7,000 square feet (650 m^2)

Auxiliary engine: 261 HP Detroit Diesel

Electrical generator: 15 KW Yanmar Diesel

Sails: Spectra Mylar, weight between 3/4 and 9 ounces

Running rigging: Braided nylon between 1/4 and 3 inches in circumference

Standing rigging: Stainless-steel wire rope between 1/4 and 2 inches in circumference

Anchors: Starboard—185-pound (83.9 kilograms) Danforth, Port—85-pound (38.5 kg) Danforth

Accommodation: 21 berths

Normal complement: One officer, four non-commissioned members, sixteen junior officers

Ship's emblem: Oriole (*Oriolus aurum*)

Built: 1921

Commissioned: 1952

The Watches

On board a ship, the day is traditionally divided into seven watches. They form the structure for basic routines: eating and sleeping.

Forenoon Watch: 0900–1200.
Usually the favourite for the "lower deckers," as they get to miss cleaning stations.

Afternoon Watch: 1200–1600.
Favoured by some because they get to knock off early for lunch. In the days of rum issue, it was sometimes difficult to function during the afternoon watch.

First Dog Watch: 1600–1800.
Usually a quiet watch. Although shorter than others, it can still be a drudgery after a long afternoon of work within one's own department.

Last Dog Watch: 1800–2000.
One of my favourites. I've always enjoyed sunset and being a navigator—a busy time for stars and astro-nav.

First Watch: 2000–2359 (Some say that 2400 does not exist In the navy).
This watch can be a drag, especially on the bridge, if there are no manoeuvres or exercises. The rest of the crew have settled into night clothing, and the nightly movie has started in the messes. The smell of popcorn throughout the ship was always pleasant. Inevitably, someone would be kind enough to bring a bowl up to the bridge with a coffee for the watch on deck.

Middle Watch: 0001–0400.
The most dreaded watch. Staying awake is always a chore. The middle watch usually means the previous afternoon was a "pipe-down," time-off for sleep.

Morning Watch: 0400–0800.
Most navigators take this watch out of choice. The dawning of a new day. Morning Civil Twilight is by far the best time for taking star sights and confirming the compass error with the sunrise. There is a real sense of waking up your world, which turns into a whirlwind of activity—almost always preplanned. I think that my watch in *Oriole* would be best signified by the morning watch.

—Lieutenant-Commander Michael J. Brooks

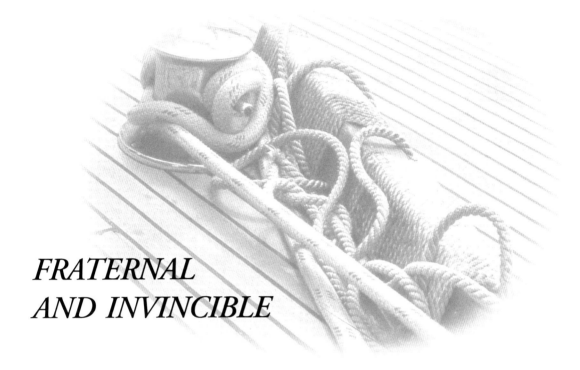

FRATERNAL
AND INVINCIBLE

Beauty and Tradition

As HMCS *Oriole* nods at her berth in Victoria's compact Inner Harbour, a tar-melting June sun sears the caulking in her teak deck. Elite high-tech yachts flank the adjacent finger floats, where a maritime ritual is ratcheting into full throttle. "Have you met Tomato?" someone asks, as a hula-skirted brunette swishes along the jetty below the granite causeway amphitheatre. Sailors, officials, wives, sweeties, and assorted friends navigate around stacked Styrofoam coolers toward the source of frying onions, where they jostle for "room at the barbie." Another queue oozes toward the hospitality boat MV *Holy Moses,* where aloha-shirted Lahaina Yacht Club hosts dispense mai tais. A couple of *bons vivants* saunter by, their hats sporting tiny pink, purple, and green paper parasols.

In the midst of all this activity, the *Oriole* stands out, awash in beauty and tradition. Her romantic bowsprit, sweeping sheerline, graceful white hull, and regal two-masted rig have captivated onlookers in many a local harbour and foreign port. As part of her sail-training and public-relations roles, the classic ketch often attends the yachting community's tribal rites, like this celebration before the 2000 Victoria-Maui International Yacht Race, which ends with a party in mid-Pacific paradise. And leaving her deck behind, resplendent in red-trimmed navy blue fleece vests, Lieutenant-Commander Scott Crawshaw and his Canadian Armed Forces crew buck the tide of multicoloured T-shirts that ebbs and flows along the docks.

HMCS Oriole *flies her genoa in the first leg of the 2000 Vic-Maui race.*

Many say Crawshaw has the best job in the navy. He captains the only commissioned yacht in the armed forces, Her Majesty's Canadian Ship *Oriole*. He brings impressive credentials to the post. Graduating in 1984 from Royal Roads Military College with a double physics and physical oceanography major, he served as deck officer and navigating officer in HMCS *Thunder, Cowichan,* and *Restigouche* and taught navigation at Esquimalt's Naval Officer Training Centre (NOTC). He was combat and training officer on board HMCS *Yukon* and operations officer in HMCS *Algonquin* before joining the Ottawa National Defence Headquarters Joint Planning Staff.

By the time Crawshaw took command of *Oriole* in August 1999, he had navigated her across 25,000 ocean miles. In 1986 and 1988, he won the Vic-Maui navigator's trophy for predicting the closest time of arrival at 25 miles. For this 2000 race, he is skipper and navigator. And while a win would be nice, it is not his priority. His goal is to perform as best he can and have a race in which he and his fledgling crew will sail all the time, have wind all the time, and have a good time doing it.

Every year, the *Oriole*'s training schedule includes an ocean race. Months before this event, Crawshaw has determined how many positions he must fill. Because *Oriole*'s main mandate is to train junior officers, the NOTC is normally his first source of students. This year, however, the Royal Military College (RMC) in Kingston, Ontario, has supplied the cadets. Most have never seen salt water. Over the next month, these bilingual trainees—four men and four women—will absorb a new vocabulary where kitchens are "galleys," ropes are "sheets," toilets are "heads," and a "shake" is a wake-up call.

Oriole's full complement—the RMC cadets, two recent female RMC grads, and twelve regular-force members, including the navy's first female electrician, Leading Seaman Dorrie Ballantyne from HMCS *Ottawa*—meet for the first time one week before the start gun sounds. Sixteen have never sailed before. Before the race, Crawshaw works up his crew, building

in a day of simulated emergencies to ensure that they will be up to speed if anything goes wrong at sea.

The Royal Vancouver Yacht Club and Maui's Lahaina Yacht Club co-sponsor this biennial 2,308-nautical-mile (nm) downwind dash. It's a race that lures sailing's "rock stars," who would dominate the podium if yacht racing were an Olympic sport. In 1978, Seattle ace Doug Fryer chartered a fast Santa Cruz 67 sloop, *Merlin,* and scored the first of his two consecutive elapsed-time victories. In 1992, Vancouver's Dan Sinclair chartered the same *Merlin* and set a Vic-Maui speed record. Four years later, Californian Roy E. Disney and his Santa Cruz 70, *Pyewacket,* shattered Sinclair's time. In 1998, Sinclair's 70-foot *Renegade* won line honours again. This year, Sinclair is back to rewrite the record book. But a

Left to right: Naden Band members Kaighin, Agopsowicz, Martin, and Smith (Petty Officers, 2nd Class) entertain from the deck of the Sail and Life Training Society (SALTS) schooner Robertson II *during the pre-race dockside festivities.*

Lahaina entry, *Grand Illusion,* shares the same goal. Their rivalry promises a duel—a race within the Race.

The Victoria waterfront is no stranger to competition. Here, rival sealing ships, clandestine rumrunners, and nineteenth-century Royal Navy midshipmen in pinnaces have paid off wagers based on speed. In 1893 the *Thermopylae* sped from here to Hong Kong in a record 23 days. Each May, some 2,000 sailors uphold this tradition when they converge for the Royal Victoria Yacht Club's Swiftsure International Yacht Race. The Vic-Maui racers will reverse the route travelled by the cargo-carrying square-rigged and clipper ships.

Sensing the potential for drama, two journalists embark as working crew. Ed Watson boards *Oriole* and prepares to relay daily voice reports back to home port and record video footage for a five-part series that will air on Vancouver Television. *National Geographic Adventurer* assigns freelance writer John Vaillant to join Sinclair on *Renegade's* sprint for a new speed record. All the pre-race attention focuses on the speedsters.

Royal Vancouver Yacht Club's Dan Sinclair (right) set a Vic-Maui speed record in 1992 and won line honours again in 1998 in his Renegade.

A Star is Born

*I*t is high noon on Tuesday, June 27, 2000. Like an elegant swan poised for flight, the 101-foot steel ketch with the tapered transom manoeuvres among the pod of eighteen snub-sterned fibreglass yachts jockeying for "room at the mark" off the Victoria waterfront. Not all are speedy sloops like *Renegade* and *Grand Illusion,* state-of-the-art ultra-light displacement boats (ULDBs) designed for fast downwind passage. Heavy boats, like *Oriole,* Doug Fryer's twenty-year-old cutter *Night Runner,* and Steve Clark's *Winds of Time,* have handicaps that give them a shot at the coveted Overall Trophy, calculated on corrected time.

Each May, the Swiftsure pits *Oriole* against the West Coast's best sailors. And every year, her loyal Victoria fans hope their "sentimental favourite" will place well, despite her age-related limitations. The Swiftsure course down Juan de Fuca Strait to the Pacific Ocean forms the first 70-nm leg of the June Vic-Maui Race. Along this volatile stretch of water, fickle winds usually scupper *Oriole*'s chances, because she needs strong, steady pressure to power her 92 tons. "Trying to get out of the Strait—that's the worst part of the whole race for *Oriole,*" Scott Crawshaw explains.

Oriole gets off to a good start. "She looked like a winner from the beginning," recalls Doug Fryer. "It's the best start I've seen *Oriole* make in 30 years

of watching her in Swiftsure. She got across the line carrying her 'chute.' Some of the smaller boats didn't make it, and got caught when the wind died."

The first tactical challenge is how to approach Race Rocks, where B.C.'s second-oldest lighthouse stands watch over Esquimalt and Victoria Harbours. Here, a navigator must decide whether to go outside the rocky outcrop or tackle the six-knot current that rips through the inner passage, spinning back eddies along the shore.

On the way to "the Race," frontrunners *Renegade* and *Grand Illusion* sail inshore by William Head and lose the wind. Pulled by her ballooning blue gennaker—the asymmetrical spinnaker set from the end of the bowsprit—*Oriole* smokes toward the black-and-white-striped tower of the lighthouse. Anticipating turquoise tropical waters, the exuberant trainees revel in their first day at sea, dangle their deck shoes over the side, raise their arms, and shout "Aloha," sending a wave from bow to stern every time they pass another yacht.

Crawshaw scans the oily surface and first decides to go outside the Race. But as the winds die and they ghost closer, he realizes they will be becalmed no matter what they do. He alters course to go inside the passage, where the tide will turn and push them through. And that is exactly what happens. Unlike in 1986 and 1988, when *Oriole* took two days to reach Cape Flattery, this year she arrives early the next morning. Dodging deep-sea vessels shrouded in a dense fog bank, the navy ketch quickly finds the offshore winds.

Sailors call Vic-Maui a "navigator's race." The North Pacific High is the wild card. Its winds rotate in a cyclonic or clockwise direction. Other high-pressure systems develop far to the west. When they come together in mid-ocean, they form a peanut shape. "It's almost like a wheel turning," explains Crawshaw. "The wheel moves positions within the Pacific and changes shape as well. What you have to do is find the right groove within that wheel. You are pretty well locked into that clockwise rotation." Navigators try to stay as far away as they can from the centre—usually located around 40° north latitude and 130 to 140° west longitude—as it can trap the unwary in a doldrums.

Before the race, Crawshaw monitored weather faxes four times a day to establish a pattern. Was the high building or decreasing? To plot course options, he chose two "way points" for reference:

30° north latitude, 140° west longitude, and 40° north latitude, 130° west longitude. This year the high is very strong and has moved a little north into the mid-40° latitudes. As the wind builds, Crawshaw abandons his game plan, heads for 30° north, and drives straight for Hawaii.

Instead of taking the traditional square-rigger route down the coast to California, *Oriole* and several other boats veer off and follow the Rhumb line, or Great Circle route. The wind rides ahead like a wave, always with a little curl, as the great ship rises and falls on the swells. The weather is ideal for *Oriole*, which doesn't happen very often on the Vic-Maui. Rather than dead astern or on the bow, the wind blows "abaft the beam" (behind the widest part of her hull). A steady 20-knot wind sweeps across her deck, angling 10-foot seas onto her quarter between the beam and stern. Flying her workhorse sail combination of main, mizzen, 1.5-ounce gennaker, and tie-dyed mizzen staysail, she coasts to Hawaii on one long tack.

The trainees learn that ocean racing is nonstop stuff. Their hands flex like the great bird's claws as they grab and release the sheets that sluice through tender palms. Although most are novice sailors, their lack of experience will not affect *Oriole*'s performance. Armed Forces personnel are disciplined to follow commands. On board a navy ship, the law decrees that they obey the captain. Automatic response ensures survival—for the ship, and for themselves.

Work, play, meals, and sleep come packaged in

Race Rocks at the eastern end of the Juan de Fuca Strait poses the first decision for the Swiftsure and Vic-Maui Race tacticians.

chunks. On the upper deck, two watch captains direct the action. Between them, coxswain (cox'n) Pat O'Hara and chief boatswain's mate (buffer, or bosun) Dave Greene have logged four Vic-Maui Races. Exempting only the captain and the cook, Don "Cookshack" Cuthbertson, they divide the crew into two groups that rotate six hours on and six hours off. While one watch sleeps, the other works the upper deck. Every other day, each watch has one six-hour shift on and two off.

On the port side of the companionway, Crawshaw's cabin doubles as cyber-command central. One laptop stores the charts. The other links with the Internet. *Oriole* is the official communications boat. Every day, as a safety check, each yacht must radio a position, which the navy crew plots on a map. As well as wind conditions and miles covered, this daily roll call circulates scuttlebutt—gossip about birthdays, anniversaries, and sea life.

In Vancouver, volunteers distill this information into a daily bulletin, which a cadet reads to the ship's company. On the second day of the race, *Grand Illusion* surges into the lead off the Oregon coast. On the fourth day, the bulletin headlines: *ORIOLE* IS TRUCKING. "The boat of the hour is undoubtedly HMCS *Oriole,* which has climbed steadily through the fleet." Covering 220 nautical miles and averaging 9.2 knots on corrected time, she leads not only the three other D Class boats, but also the entire fleet. As flat grey seas blur into leaden skies, the frontrunners have already outdistanced *Merlin*'s and *Pyewacket*'s record runs, indicating a fast race and a possible new record.

Doug Fryer and his *Night Runner* crew keep *Oriole* in sight for several days. "In a fluky patch, we saw her with no headsails up doing spinnaker drills four days out in the horse lats at the beginning of the squalls," Fryer recalls.

HMCS Oriole *Commanding Officer Lieutenant-Commander Scott Crawshaw holds three trophies for the Vic-Maui navigator with the nearest ETA at 25-mile call-in.*

But Crawshaw decides against using the symmetrical spinnaker, because it is not worth the risk for a small gain. On a cloudy night with no moonlight, it is very difficult to fly this "chute" without any horizon reference point. More important, properly setting this sail with its heavy pole takes repeated practice. Cadets normally come on board for one or two weeks; it usually takes them that long to learn how to fly this huge sail.

On July 1, only leaders *Grand Illusion* and *Renegade* better *Oriole*'s daily run. Steven Tuck's *Darby* crew scoops a large glass fishing float and startles a dozing whale, which spins a phosphorescent circle around them. Other yachts pick hitchhiking squid off the deck and dine on freshly caught tuna.

Oriole's "morale centre" calculates menus long before she goes offshore. For this voyage, she carries a three-week supply of food and water. Cuthbertson presides over the tiny galley tucked between the wardroom and the focs'le (bow). Fresh produce like green-tipped bananas and lettuce keeps for three days in the refrigerator's bottom cooler; four-gallon milk jugs and other perishables fill the top section. Cans occupy bins under the captain's and cox'n's cabins on each side of the companionway.

Water is precious. On the way to Hawaii, the crew consumes 60 cases of half-litre bottles, 24 to a flat. Under the wardroom deck, a chest freezer holds ice packs for treating sunstroke. A reverse-osmosis machine generates water for chores. "Pot wallopers" wash dishes in salt water and rinse with fresh.

"Heaven creates food. Hell cooks it," comments Cuthbertson. He labours in temperatures that hover between 100° and 125°F and copes by wrapping sweat-stopping bandanas around his forehead and neck. To keep hydrated he drinks two dozen glasses of water every day, at fifteen-minute intervals. Night brings no relief from this sauna: The cook's bunk hugs the starboard hull beside the stove. Before he goes on deck, Cuthbertson bundles his six-foot frame into longjohns and long sleeves so he won't get chilled.

Ocean racers can burn 5,000 calories over 24 hours. Granola bars, chocolate bars, flavoured rice cakes, and packaged cookies are handy snacks. To keep the crew's blood-sugar levels pumped, 'Shack plans nutritious menus. Breakfasts offer heat-holding scrambled eggs and pancakes, as well as packaged dry cereal, yogurt, and instant oatmeal. Lunch is soup and sandwiches. Cheese is a staple. High-protein casseroles like tuna win over sauces because they don't fly upward when served. "When you are doing a dance in the ocean," says Cuthbertson, "nothing stays still."

Cooking at an angle is a constant challenge, especially when that angle rotates through a large arc. Whenever the ship tacks, Cuthbertson keeps an ear tuned for the sail master's call on the deck above his head: "Report to tacking stations." Someone always shouts down, "Ready on the stove."

July 5 is a special day. To celebrate the captain's birthday, 'Shack emerges on deck bearing a special confection. Crawshaw's wife Sonia and his daughters Alexandria and Katrina have smuggled a chocolate cake mix and party hats on board. Baking requires ingenuity, because the stove is hotter on one side than the other. To compensate, Cuthbertson turns pans around halfway through their baking time. Another birthday happens on the Pacific rollers when the youngest cadet turns nineteen. But Francesca Lussier misses out on the traditional toast. When she is sailing, the *Oriole* is a dry ship.

Mary Coakley is the only civilian on board. On shore in the admiral's office, her work with personnel hones her observation skills. She tells of the learning curves mastered, especially as the crew struggles to tie up the spinnaker and gennaker in readiness for the next hoist. "It was interesting to watch eleven people fight for two feet of space to tie as many knots as they could instead of developing an efficient system," she recalls. "But this crew learned quickly and developed teamwork in a very short time."

The petite grandmother marvels at the incredible sense of isolation one feels when the ship is the only visible speck in a vast circle of ocean. But the elements bring a profound sense of peace. At night, gentle shudders run down the hull, and the sails sing a lullaby. Alert to sounds, she wakes up and thinks, "Okay. We are still making good speed." The ocean dissolves distractions that on land can block a stream of consciousness, allowing her to plumb new depths of feelings, thoughts, and dreams. On night watch, she practises yoga. Then, by moonlight, her fingers guide a grease pen over

The Vic-Maui 2000 crew takes a mid-ocean break.

the plastic chart cover as she composes poems about sibilant sounds and cobalt seas—and hopes no one erases them before dawn.

On the seventh day, *Grand Illusion* maintains a 70-nm lead with a 278-nm run. The navy crew logs another 206 nautical miles to remain first in class and first overall. *Oriole*'s Canadian Forces Sailing Association (CFSA) clubmate Al Byers and his *Windshadow X* crew have some fun and report sighting "a Swiss aircraft carrier, an albatross with the ancient mariner around its neck, and three dolphins playing catch with a big red ball." On the eighth day out, *Oriole* stretches her class lead with a 209-nm run, bested only by the two "rocket ships," *Renegade* and *Grand Illusion*.

In the last few days before Hawaii, the greenish turquoise sea turns black. Rain buckets onto *Oriole*'s deck. "You can't see five feet in front of you, and hope there's nobody there," says Dave Greene. When he was driving, "Buff" de-powered the ship by pinching her bow up into the wind. "We were honking," he says. Squalls, caused when hot air rises, cools, and drops, start showing up on the radar. As this air picks up momentum, it shoots forward and creates a phenomenal gust. A typical 20- to 25-knot trade wind increases to 40 or 50 knots. "Each squall cell is almost like a little low-pressure system," says Crawshaw. "It's got its own weather. The ones we saw were about five to ten miles apart."

Playing the squalls is an important tactic. Boats like *Renegade* chase the wind where it is greatest and gybe to stay inside as long as they can harness the power. *Oriole* can't do that because she doesn't move fast enough to bring her stern through the wind for a gybe that will get her into the right location. "We play the edge of the squall," says Crawshaw. "It's almost by guess and by golly, and good luck if the right edge happens to come over you."

As the squalls pass, it's almost as if they suck all the energy out of the atmosphere. For a little while there will be nothing, until the trades pick up again or another squall comes through. A squall hits *Oriole*. As it passes, the wind dies. The trainees use the slack time to play "Twister" on deck for a couple of hours.

The navigator's final critical decision is when to gybe onto the port tack and complete the last few days to Maui. Crawshaw explains, "If you tack too soon, you end up pointing too far downwind. This slows the boat and increases the chance of an accidental gybe. Gybing too late adds more miles." He calculates several gybe vectors, and when the weather prognosis shows a ridge of high pressure forming southeast of the North Pacific High, it means that the wind is going to veer a bit.

After a blistering 341-nm run, the first boat surfs across the finish line on July 6, 2000. A media release announces: "Skippered by James McDowell of Redondo Beach, California, the Santa Cruz 70 *Grand Illusion* arrived in Maui after nine days and two hours at sea, slicing seventeen hours off *Pyewacket*'s 1996 record."

"This race has been a terrific combination of sportsmanship and adventure," says David Williams, managing partner of event-title and *Oriole* sponsor PricewaterhouseCoopers. "Not only is it an exciting race, but it also involves the Victoria community, many of whom are following the race with avid interest. More than 1,600 people are subscribing to daily race reports by e-mail."

On July 7, *Renegade* romps home, also besting *Pyewacket*'s former record. "We hit speeds of more than 20 knots so many times you couldn't count them," exults Dan Sinclair.

Tropical fragrances waft 30 miles out to sea, tantalizing weary crews who have planed for days on ten-foot waves. And while superbly conditioned athletes back home pack their passports for the upcoming 2000 Summer Olympic Games, an unheralded Canadian "dream team"—23 amateur sailors with the stamina of international soccer players—pulls off a sporting coup in the course of its working day.

On Tuesday, July 10, 2000, at 04:00:19 HST, a firework bursts in an ebony sky to welcome the seventh boat across the finish line. After twelve days, nineteen hours, and nineteen seconds at sea, HMCS *Oriole* has beaten out twelve faster B and C Class competitors boat for boat, winning the prestigious Royal Vancouver Yacht Club Trophy for first overall on corrected time. Teamwork vaults the navy yacht into the elite constellation of ocean-racing royals. And a new star is born.

Lahaina's dredged harbour is too shallow for *Oriole*'s ten-foot draft. By the time the morning watch ties up to the United States Coast Guard buoy, bags the sails, and organizes the deck lines, dawn's first fingers streak the sky. Crawshaw endures the ritual skipper dunking. Then representatives from PricewaterhouseCoopers and the Lahaina Yacht Club whisk the victors away in a small boat to the traditional welcome luau, replete with flower leis, mai tais, champagne, and food. Those on the duty watch miss this custom of sponsors greeting each yacht after it crosses the finish line, but the next day's arrivals quickly absorb them into their own dock parties.

The race committee uses computer simulation from U.S. Sailing's Rhode Island office to calculate handicaps. Performance factors supply predictions that are applied to a race weather model based on previous race conditions. This gives a single predicated performance number for each boat, specifically tailored to its predicted Vic-Maui race conditions. Some post-mortems question *Oriole*'s handicap, but because she has competed almost every year since the race began in 1968, it can be argued that her 140 rating is probably the most accurate of all the yachts.

This race has educated the trainees on two levels. When something goes wrong under sail, the crew must react instinctively and as a team. Teamwork develops rapidly on the upper deck, because everyone absorbs a collective experience at the same time in the same small space. A gut feel for wind and sea conditions and their potential impact can be transferred to any ship. Even a destroyer can be damaged under certain sea conditions. Grasping a sense of the power of the sea is a lesson that will last forever, after victory celebrations have become a fond memory.

On the return voyage, the cadets internalize individual lessons, as continuous stress sears new psychological insights into their psyches. They get a crash course in the first maxim every mariner learns, "One hand for the ship, and one hand for yourself." As *Oriole*'s bow slams into walls of hard waves, water cascades over the deck and seeps into their bunks. Cookshack braces himself in the galley. Dishwashers wear safety harnesses and strap themselves to the portholes. Crockery flies and crashes. The cadets dream about mundane

---

HMCS *Oriole* collects five prizes

- The Royal Vancouver Yacht Club Trophy for first overall—corrected time
- Class D first to finish
- Class D first overall
- Andreas Schueller Memorial Trophy for navigator with the nearest ETA at 25-mile call-in for Lieutenant-Commander Scott Crawshaw, his third
- Byrd Award for the crew having too much fun

---

landlubber comforts. Beds that don't move. More variety in food and drink.

On August 11, 2000, HMCS *Oriole* sails a victory run along the Victoria waterfront. An Aurora aircraft weaves vapour trails as the Canadian navy's longest-serving ship leaves the familiar Duntze Head landmark to starboard and motors toward her narrow jetty, which is jammed with family and friends. As the Comox Sea Cadet Band strikes up a spirited "Heart of Oak," Rear-Admiral Ron Buck, Commander, Maritime Forces Pacific, steps forward and grabs a mooring line. *Oriole*'s sponsors are there to present each crew member with a souvenir: a navy blue fleece vest embroidered in turquoise letters:

1st

VIC MAUI 2000

PRICEWATERHOUSECOOPERS

HMCS ORIOLE

Training
Adventures

Two months have passed since the Vic-Maui race, and I find myself helping to crew HMCS *Oriole*. An autumn sun splashes diamonds across Esquimalt Harbour as she slips and leaves Duntze Head to port. Twelve military career counsellors from Canadian Armed Forces recruiting centres in Edmonton, Vancouver, and Victoria have volunteered to "pull strings" on this Adventure Training Cruise to the American Gulf Islands in September 2000. These regular-force officers have four days to work up into a team that responds automatically and efficiently to the tasks on the upper deck.

I am the only civilian. I've stuffed my tape recorder, notepad, and extra film into my jacket pocket and slung my ubiquitous Nikon around my neck. Of the six core crew, all but the cook have Vic-Maui tales to tell. I was honorary commodore for Captain Scott Crawshaw's first community event, the 1999 Classic Boat Festival. I know the cox'n and buffer from the festival sailpast three weeks ago.

The *Oriole* and I have been CFSA clubmates since 1963. And although it was back in May 1968, I still remember the first time I stepped on board. My feet wore shocking-pink fabric shoes. I must have been trying to impress the tall, blond captain, Geoffrey Hilliard, who had invited me for lunch to talk about

the first Vic-Maui race for my weekly *Victoria Times* column, "Around Our Shores."

Today, my grey dinghy boots sheath grey wool socks. I can predict our first drill. Leading Seaman Andy Sage shepherds us below in small groups. Aware of the dire consequences if we don't, we dutifully memorize the 5-21-5 sequence that pumps the head in the cox'n and buffer's cabin on the starboard side of the companionway.

Safety comes first. Buffer Dave Greene reminds us that we have to look out for one another. Twenty minutes after we leave the jetty, the captain throws our orange kisby ring, Oscar, overboard, catapulting the crew into a Man Overboard Exercise (MOBEX). A fluorescent flag follows, marking Oscar's position. Speed is the key. Log entries tell the story:

> 1005: Verification muster correct.
> 1006: Launched sea boat.
> 1007: Man out of water.
> 1008: Recovered MOB marker.
> 1009: Recovered sea boat.

As we motor eastward toward Trial Island's lighthouse, the "string-pullers" wedge themselves toboggan-style along the port guardrail. Here, Chief Warrant Officer Tom P. "Chowder" Chauder,

Edmonton 411 vehicle technician, waits. And dreams of wind. Enough wind to bury the turquoise scupper that runs along his thigh, scoop up the heaving sea, and funnel it down the narrow teak alley between the coach house and the guardrail. A roller-coaster return from Hawaii the month before prompts a reality check from "Stokes," engineer Jason Turner. "Enough wind is exciting for the first half-hour," he opines. "After that, it's hard work."

Short, fit, former navy diver Greene pads purposefully up and down the deck in his running shoes as he fires questions. "This is a mainsheet. Why do you call it a mainsheet?"

A male voice fires back, "It's on the mainsail."

"There you go. Now you're thinking," Buff confirms. "That's how it works. This one here brings the boom in and out. Sheets trim the sail. Any other questions?"

He continues, "This is the position you take when you haul in on the rope. You guys will learn later what point of sail we are on. I'll say, 'Heave in on the sheets,' or I'll say, 'Aft the sheets.' Start pulling it in. Okay? TWO AND SIX HEAVE. TWO AND SIX HEAVE. Everybody lean forward, and you go HEAVE, hand over hand. Ready? Let's go! When I'm standing here, if I see you're having trouble

A fire drill starts every new training session. Leading Seaman Jason Turner mans the pump that sucks sea water, which is combined with a liquid to form a fire-resistant foam that is sprayed on any flame. Lieutenant (N) Cynthia Nadeau dons a fire-retardant uniform that protects skin against flame or explosion. When Oriole *is alongside her jetty, a heat sensor connects her to the Dockyard Fire Department, which is 300 yards away.*

Buffer Dave Greene oversees Corporal Helen Goldie and crew after gennaker takedown.

"How long did that take? Like I said, if the skipper wants to tack, he wants to go ten minutes ago. Okay? It takes a lot of time for *Oriole* to get ready to tack. It takes 30 seconds to do it. I can't have a foul-up in the middle of it, because that's when stuff happens. This is why we practise. Okay? As we go, you're going to get better at it. The first couple are going to be dicey. I know that. You learn by your mistakes. Nobody's perfect. Just keep aware. If you're gonna say you're ready, make sure you're ready."

One of the women asks, "What happens if we're not?"

"Oh, I'll wait for ya," he replies. "But I can't wait forever, or I'll get in there and do it myself. Sage is on the foredeck. You'll hear me say 'and a good foredeck guy would have got that through.' The foresail always gets caught. Once we have done our tack and cleaned up the mess, then we can relax.

"I pick three strapping lads. Once you get the mainsail all the way up, I'm gonna say, 'Swingers take the weight.'"

The gals laugh. Buff continues.

"I'm gonna say to you guys, 'Hands up.' Put your hands up in the air. That tells me that nobody's hangin' on to it. Okay? Where's Ritchie? You're gonna go down and take the main purchase at the end."

Satisfied that we're sufficiently primed, Buff calls to the bridge, "Turn her into the wind."

Above the engine vibration, Crawshaw yells, "You ready?"

Concentration registers on every face as the mainsail slides up the 104-foot fir mainmast. Greene's commands crescendo: "Haul away. AFT! AFT! HEAVE! HEAVE! Get her up! PUT YER BACK INTO IT! Come on!! Two and six HEAVE!!! ONE FOR THE QUEEN!!!! HEAVE!!!!! SWINGERS TAKE THE WEIGHT!!!!!!"

The motor cuts out. Tiny bubbles sizzle in *Oriole*'s wake as the sails start to power us in the

hanging on to it, I'll say, 'Up and out.' You can let go of it. Don't go anywhere."

We learn that we must be vigilant when we are walking around the deck. We could trip over a cleat, sheet, or block and tackle. Things move. Lines roll under your feet. "A rope has a mind of its own," Buff tells us. "You never, EVER wrap a line around your hand, around your arm, around your leg. NEVER. When the sails load up there's an amazing amount of pressure."

Buff ratchets up the pace. "Ready about, Skipper. AYE. AYE. Helm's a-lee. Away we GO. Jigger down your backstays. Let fly. Break your backstays. Aft the sheet. That quick," he volleys.

light air. One critical tacking manoeuvre requires precise teamwork. Otherwise, the mast can pull out. Stainless-steel running backstays absorb tension in the masts. When *Oriole* is sailing, one backstay is always loose. Its counterpart on the other side of the hull is always tight. They are made up of two parts: the main purchase and the block and tackle. Under tension, the lines become bar-taut. It takes twelve people, three on each side of the main and mizzen, to "make" (tighten) and "break" (loosen) the backstays as the ship swings her bow through the wind.

The commanding officer's command "Buffer, ready about" activates the sequence for our first starboard tack, when the port backstays are being made up. (The main purchases are made up automatically, and when the person on the cleat reports "Ready," it means he or she is ready to jigger the backstays down.)

"Tacking stations," yells the buffer. "Centre the main and mizzen. Make up your backstays. Report from the high side."

Assistant Sail Master Sage's "Ready on the foredeck" triggers a chain response of "Ready" from the people standing by at the cleats for the jumbo and the Yankee sheets, followed rapidly by:

"Ready on the starboard main backstay."

"Ready on the starboard mizzen backstay."

"Ready on the port mizzen backstay."

"Ready on the port main backstay."

"Ready to let fly Yankee."

"Ready to let fly jumbo."

"Ready about, sir," calls the buffer.

"Helm's a-lee," shouts the commanding officer.

As *Oriole* reaches the point when her bow goes through the wind, she will no longer heel. Buff orders, "Jigger down your backstays!" He watches to see that the port backstay jiggers are turned up (cleated), then informs the commanding officer

that they are made up. It is now safe to go through the wind.

When we are "head to wind," the buffer yells, "LET FLY!" Sage watches the foresails and sheets to make sure they go around the forestay. As the sail starts to come around, Buff orders those on the sheets to take up some of the slack. Now our bow is through the wind. "BREAK YOUR STARBOARD BACKSTAYS." Then he calls out, "Aft the sheet" to those hauling on the Yankee sheet.

The port backstay crew members have finished their task and are back on the sheets. When the Yankee sheet slack is paid out, Buff returns to the familiar "TWO, SIX, HEAVE." As soon as the sail is set and drawing, he commands, "WELL ON THE SHEET, TURN UP."

Crawshaw identifies the instruments at his compact helm station:

"On the bridge I have a handheld GPS. The hard-wired GPS system is in my cabin. This radar display is a slave to the one in my cabin; whatever shows on the radar in my cabin is displayed on the screen here. Also, the radar is hooked to the GPS in my cabin so that I can display latitude and longitude on the radar screen, as well as the radar picture. Here is the depth sounder; the engine instruments that show temperature, revolutions, and oil pressure; the emergency engine shut-off switch; sailing instruments (three NEXUS displays for wind, and two multi-displays for course and boat speed); VHF marine radio (all marine channels); binnacle; engine throttle; fire extinguisher; emergency alarm button to activate a bell throughout the boat. Near the helm are two Man Overboard poles with strobes attached (one on either side), two Man Overboard smoke markers with strobes, and three kisby rings, one with a drogue and strobe attached. When we go offshore, I also bring a device called a SART (Search and Rescue Transponder). I throw it overboard if someone falls in, and it sends a signal that shows up on the radar, so I can return to the spot at night or in rough seas. This is extremely important if someone was to fall overboard when sailing downwind with a chute up in a heavy sea. It would take about five to ten minutes to return to the spot."

"On," shouts Jason Turner. (The person on the cleat is always one of the core crew.)

Our final command tells us that the commanding officer and buffer are satisfied with the sail trim. "UP AND OUT, CLEAN UP THE MESS" rewards us for a successful tack. Now we can relax for a while.

Crawshaw tells us how *Oriole*'s core crew members are chosen for their leadership skills and their ability to motivate others—and make it fun. Typically, the engineer and the cook will have zero experience on board the training ketch. On the upper deck, Crawshaw tries to get a leading seaman to come in, usually as the assistant sail master. This person rotates off the *Oriole* to another posting, then comes back to her as the buffer, who looks after "strings and things"—sails and their repair.

The cox'n and buffer are petty officer positions. Both serve as primary watch captain. Dave Greene was an Ottawa Sea Cadet who joined the navy in 1981 and drove crash boats at Alberta's CFB Cold Lake before he came to Esquimalt. The buffer advances to cox'n, who looks after "beds and heads"—paperwork, stores, crew discipline, and morale. Pat O'Hara first sailed in *Oriole* on a Swiftsure with Bill Walker. A stint at HMCS Cornwallis preceded his fifth posting to the ketch.

We overnight at Port Sidney Marina. The next morning, we ghost up the Haro Strait between Canada and the United States, keeping a weather eye out for tide lines and wind shifts. Buffer rides herd on his acolytes. Mostly, he praises. But one glitch invokes a previous cox'n—"Lascelle would turn over in his grave if he could see you guys." (A new glass-and-concrete building by Naden's small-boat jetty bears his name.)

Sage hands out short lengths of rope for knot-tying practice, telling us which one makes the best handle for a skipping rope. Soon we have mastered

bowlines and clove hitches, and we tie them behind our backs as a test.

Underway, the *Oriole* resembles a closed ecosystem that quickly develops its own distinct rhythms, routines, and mythology. A crucible that transforms disparate souls into "shipmates"—that special bond that can only be experienced and can perhaps never completely be understood by others. The largest group of career counsellors comes from Vancouver. Luc rarely emerges from the galley, where he is helping Leading Seaman Norm "Cookshack" Vermette prepare food for us. When Chris is off-watch, he buries his nose in a paperback. Fred cracks us up with his off-the-wall one-liners. Cynthia never misses an opportunity to hitch a hoist up the mainmast in the bosun's chair. At the chart table, Jennifer, an NOTC Venture graduate who works in HMC Dockyard, plots tracks and logs GPS and other notations on a small notepad. For whatever reason, every time there's a takedown, it's the ladies who line up along the boom to scoop and secure the sail: Monique, Marg, Tanya, my watch mate Teresa, and Helen.

Off Salmon Bank at the south end of San Juan Island, we collect on the foredeck, where O'Hara and Greene drill us in the intricacies of setting the spinnaker. Sounding like machine-gun fire, a staccato burst of pops releases the sail ties, and some 7,000 square feet of Dacron billow in the gentle breeze. After lunch, we cross the invisible border into Washington State. Like the Pied Piper, the *Oriole* attracts retinues wherever she travels. As we secure alongside Friday Harbor Marina, backpackers waiting for the float plane to Seattle wander over to check us out. Some catch this Kodak moment. Others ask about the Vic-Maui Race.

By Thursday afternoon, the predicted clouds clothe the dark-green island humps. Late afternoon finds us alongside the floats at Rosario Resort on

Chief Warrant Officer Tom Chauder and Corporal Tanya Shier feed a cormorant that hitched a ride to dry out his feathers between Rosario Resort and Victoria's Baynes Channel.

Orcas Island. On the foredeck, O'Hara replays the Vic-Maui triumph for an attentive couple and their golden Lab dog. He explains that night driving requires concentration. "You have to be up there 25 or 30 minutes before you take over the wheel to let your night vision get settled and get the intimidation factor down." Before anyone goes ashore for showers, we sort out this night's rotation with watch captain Norm Vermette.

Midnight sticks to me. Bulked up in clammy, yellow, wet-weather jacket and overalls, I waddle up the companionway to the rain-lashed deck. Someone has jury-rigged a coat hanger to spread the deep flaps of the blue mainsail cover. Huddled on the coachhouse roof under this makeshift shelter, my face pressed against the reassuring smoothness of the varnished boom crutch, I assess the storm. The wind is building. I think I hear a snort, so I scan the blackness with my flashlight. Nothing. Later, this bay will seethe with whitecaps. I wonder idly if this weather will hold long enough for "Chowder" to realize his dream for lots of wind.

At the top of every hour, the duty watch makes its rounds. Checks all the mooring lines. Climbs down the vertical iron ladder to "Tiller Flats" below the bridge. Checks for water in the bilge. Checks the engine room to make sure that the amps needle is registering more than zero and two green lights are glowing. My wet-weathers rasp as I shuffle downstairs to the dimly lit wardroom's gimballed table and make my 0100 log "rounds correct" entry. I use pencil—ink runs if it gets wet.

I return to my dripping perch and gear my mind to idle. After decades of "welcome aboards," being charged with the responsibility for *Oriole*'s welfare deepens my bond with this gently rocking cradle. The dark and the storm cocoon us. Locked into a time warp, isolated and insulated from past and future tense, I marvel at how completely the present expands to block out everything but the "now."

The next morning is Friday, September 29. As we cast off, a sullen sea and brooding sky shroud the ship, foreshadowing this day's place in history. O'Hara hands the helm to Edmonton naval lieutenant Pat Leslie for our uneventful reach across Haro Strait to Victoria. A light drizzle mists *Oriole* as we power past Duntze Head. In a final on-board ritual, the crew lines up along the starboard guardrail, shortest to tallest, hands behind backs. Buffer shrills two tones on the bosun's pipe. The trainees snap to attention. As we motor slowly down the line of warships, dark-blue figures return the salute. On every slate-grey stern, a white ensign sags at half-mast. I turn to the commanding officer and ask why.

Back home, I turn on the telly; a national news anchor is eulogizing a former prime minister who I met in the 1970s. "A nation in search of a collective ritual will soon be awash in a collective outpouring of grief."

Pierre Elliott Trudeau is dead.

Trudeau was neither the last nor the first Canadian prime minister to be hosted on board an *Oriole* yacht. When HMCS *Oriole* represented the Royal Canadian Navy at Quebec's 1984 tall ships events, he was the guest of Lieutenant-Commander James Gracie. In Pearl Harbor in 1997, Lieutenant-Commander Michael Brooks entertained Kim Campbell, elected in 1993 as Canada's first and only female prime minister. Their visits echoed the hospitality extended by Royal Canadian Yacht Club commodore George Gooderham to the Dominion of Canada's first prime minister, Sir John A. Macdonald, on board the *Oriole II* in 1888. Hosting royalty and high-ranking politicians has its roots in the nineteenth-century traditions established by what some have called "Canada's sporting royalty"—the Gooderham family.

IN THE BEGINNING

Toujours en Avant

*I*n the beginning, Little Trinity on Toronto's East King Street was called "Gooderham's church," in honour of its main benefactor. When its congregation held its first service on Valentine's Day, 1844, Little Trinity was the second Anglican church in a growing community of 17,000. Now the oldest church building in Toronto, the neo-Gothic structure is dominated by its original 60-foot bell tower, buttressed on each corner. The pointed window arches, baptismal font, and Tudor-style chairs have not changed.

As today's commemoratives confirm, the Gooderham name will always have a place here. Most prominent are the marbled memorials that honour the founders. "Full of years and honours, William Gooderham of Scole, Norfolk, England died on

August 20th, 1881 aged 91 years. Mark the perfect man and behold the upright, for the end of that man is peace." And "Harriet Gooderham of Sipton, Suffolk, England. A devoted wife, affectionate mother, and humble believer in the Lord Jesus Christ."

Faith and family formed the foundation for the Gooderhams' enterprises and sustained the social responsibility ingrained in their sturdy souls. The saga began in 1831, with an exodus from the edge of the North Sea. William Gooderham's brother-in-law, James Worts, shepherded 54 men, women, and children related by blood or marriage on board a ship bound for the New World. Worts, a successful miller, and his wife Sarah settled where he could harness the full force of Lake Ontario's prevailing winds. At "Muddy York," he built a grist mill out of limestone carried from Kingston as ship's ballast.

William Gooderham was a farmer who had served with the British Army in the West Indies. In 1832, he sailed to Canada with his wife Harriet and family. They arrived with eleven children orphaned during the voyage and raised them with seven of their own. Gooderham deposited almost 2,000 pounds in the Bank of Upper Canada, the largest single deposit recorded to that point in the bank's history.

On July 27, 1832, he formed a partnership with Worts. Before long, their pioneer mill was supplying most of the rural hinterland's flour and livestock feed. Many farmers bartered large amounts of grain for milling services. Not wanting to waste the liquefied mash left over from the process, the thrifty partners looked for ways to recycle it. They soon realized that surplus and second-rate grain could turn a higher profit as alcohol than as feed for their dairy herds.

By the time James Worts died in 1834, the mill was selling more than 1,000 gallons of spirits annually. At 50 cents a gallon, Lower Canada residents and innkeepers consumed it in ever-growing quantities. William Gooderham converted the entire operation to a distillery, where whisky production soared to 28,000 domestic and export gallons; some of the profits went to Bishop John Strachan's Little Trinity church project.

In 1845, James Gooderham Worts joined his uncle and cemented the trademark partnership Gooderham & Worts. By the end of the nineteenth century, the tall smokestacks rising from their brick factory complex dominated the skyline of Toronto's new industrial district. Gooderham & Worts was now producing one third of all the proof spirits distilled in Canada. To feed the great vats, thousands of bushels of grain arrived via trading schooners and a narrow-gauge spur of the new Grand Trunk Railway.

The first name recorded in Little Trinity's book of christenings is William Gooderham's son Charles. Charles's brother George would become most prominent in the business, but the entire family was involved in the community. While their husbands and fathers made capital contributions, wives and daughters volunteered for charitable work. The patriarch who expanded the family portfolio into railways and insurance was also a philanthropist who funded a wing of Toronto General Hospital and donated land to support his church. From 1864 until his death seventeen years later, William was president of the Bank of Toronto.

William's third son, George, succeeded his father as company president in 1881. With an unassuming integrity and quiet dignity, he too influenced Toronto's business community as president of the Bank of Toronto, director of Toronto General Trust, and member of the harbour board. Reputed to be one of Ontario's wealthiest men, George Gooderham accumulated vast tracts of land, some 150 residences, and many commercial buildings. At the corner where Wellington and Front Streets meet Church Street, George built the landmark Gooderham Flatiron Building for his head office in 1892. Ontario newspapers lamented his death in 1905 as "a public loss."

But all was not industry in George Gooderham's world. Lake Ontario, central Canada's yachting crucible, caressed the factory foreshore within hailing distance of the Gooderhams' Trinity Street homes. The wind-conscious clan turned to Toronto Bay for sport and recreation at the world's largest freshwater sailing club, the Royal Canadian Yacht Club (RCYC).

The RCYC and Gooderham names are almost inseparable. And inextricably linked with both of those names is another: *Oriole.* "Every Torontonian, every Ontario man, has heard of the *Oriole*," wrote archivist C. H. J. Snider in the 1937 *RCYC Annals.*

"No matter how scanty his knowledge of yachting, if he has any idea at all, it includes the *Oriole*, usually Gooderham's *Oriole*. The name has been associated with the Gooderham family for as long as they have been associated with yachting … They were centres of hospitality from the day they kissed the waves of Lake Ontario."

A judge and two other RCYC members formed a syndicate and commissioned the first *Oriole* in 1871 from a Maltese shipwright who built commercial vessels on the Welland Canal. A New York pilot-boat architect drew the lines for the beamy, shallow-draft, centreboard schooner, a popular design for lake cruising. The 76-foot *Oriole* often cruised with Toronto's professional and social elite on board for day sails. One cruise took her to a Chicago family's summer home in the Thousand Islands, where visiting guests Lieutenant-General Philip H. Sheridan and Ulysses S. Grant inscribed the ship's log with crossed American and Canadian flags and the notation: "The two flags and the two countries. May they be always fraternal as they are invincible." Before iron ribbons linked remote outposts, the *Oriole* poked an exploratory bowsprit into Gulf of St. Lawrence anchorages and Hudson's Bay Company forts that rimmed Lake Superior's wilderness.

On both sides of the border, the newly organized Lake Yacht Racing Association (LYRA) circuit connected many isolated communities. Sailors cruised to a rendezvous, raced, then cruised to the next destination. For competition, the syndicate painted *Oriole*'s hull with black lead to the covering board and added a square sail to catch more wind. These "go-fast" tricks paid off when their pride won the prestigious Prince of Wales Cup five times in six years.

The Gooderham name was synonymous with progress, stability, and continuity in Toronto's cultural, social, and business communities. In 1884, possibly seeking new challenges, George Gooderham looked to his waterfront. What could be more progressive than owning the finest yacht in the fleet, with bragging rights to an impressive racing record? RCYC Vice-Commodore George Gooderham bought *Oriole*.

Meanwhile, two of his sons shared his love of a good race. From the same St. Catharines shipyard that had launched his father's newly acquired schooner, *Oriole*, William Gooderham ordered an opposite design. His *Aileen* was a plumb-bowed English cutter, deep, narrow, and heavy. Cruising and racing together, father and son transferred family solidarity onto the water. George's second son, Albert, founder of the Toronto Symphony, sometimes joined the pair in *Cleopatra*, considered the finest steam yacht afloat.

On August 2, 1885, disaster struck on land and lake. As an easterly gale lathered Niagara Bar, *Aileen* and *Oriole* departed hastily at midnight to check an ominous blaze on the horizon. The flames that illuminated the Toronto waterfront guided the reefed yachts as they plunged through the wildest night any sailor could remember. The inferno levelled the Esplanade and a seven-storey sugar refinery—Toronto's tallest building, partly owned by the Gooderhams. Worse, the wild passage opened *Oriole*'s planks. Spewing oakum, she limped into Whitby Harbour. High repair estimates led George to reluctantly have her chopped up rather than sold for a freight scow. But George Gooderham was not long without a boat.

Oriole II was launched in 1886. She swung on a mooring at the foot of Sherbourne Street, and on many a fine summer afternoon she would weigh anchor and go "junketing." Prominent businessmen and politicians—sometimes accompanied by their wives and daughters—signed her guest log. In 1888,

George Gooderham, seen here at the wheel of the first Oriole. *The second* Oriole's *logbook, with this August 4, 1886, entry, is a Gooderham family treasure. "Toronto, 4th September, 1886. The ship yard at the foot of Parliament Street presented a gay appearance this afternoon being the occasion of the launching of Mr. George Gooderham's new yacht, the* Oriole ... *the handsome craft resplendent with flags and bunting from stem to stern."*

the ship's cannon saluted Prime Minister Sir John A. Macdonald and his party of eighteen when they boarded for a luncheon outing. Before auxiliary power was available, dying winds often becalmed sailboats, so Gooderham acquired a small steam launch to tow her.

As he pursued trophies with characteristic zest, George Gooderham introduced an amateur element into a sport that had been dominated by professionals. Gooderham or one of his sons usually took the helm. Otherwise, Captain Dick Fugler, the professional skipper of the first *Oriole*, directed the four paid hands who worked the sails. To reduce windage during international races, he often ordered every man flat on the deck and flat on his face.

As they campaigned their blue-and-white-checkered Gooderham house flag up and down the Great Lakes, the Gooderhams often travelled 1,200 miles for a single regatta. Bets usually rode on the outcome of every race, with men sometimes wagering land as well as coin. Between 1886 and 1892, *Oriole II* captured the Prince of Wales Challenge Cup six times, and the Marquis of Lorne Cup twice. In 1888, when Gooderham was the RCYC commodore, he accepted an invitation to race for an international trophy presented by the Hotel Plant at Mackinac Island in the Straits of Mackinac, which lie between Lake Michigan and Lake Huron. Leaving Toronto on August 2, *Oriole* sailed the whole way, a round trip of 1,300 miles, and returned on August 25 bearing the Mackinac Cup. The 23 days included dry-docking in Detroit to have her bottom sanded and black-leaded. She then defeated the Chicago America's Cup defender

Idler and the Cleveland schooner *Wasp* on both elapsed and corrected time.

The eighth of George Gooderham's sons, George Horace, was a consummate purveyor of initiative and enterprise. George Horace promoted trends that accelerated change on road and water. Born on April 18, 1868, he learned the distilling business from the ground up. As a young man he sometimes worked the night shift, which required that he stir the vats every hour. Before nodding off to sleep, the ever-enterprising George Horace tied a string around his big toe and instructed the watchman to yank it on his rounds to wake him up.

After the First World War, Gooderham & Worts' market share increased steadily, and the company became the largest distillery in the British Empire. Peacetime brought American prohibition, which leveraged Canadian distillery profits exponentially. From 1918 until 1927, when the operation was sold to Hiram Walker, Gooderham & Worts commanded a global distribution with no export competition coming from the 48 states to the south.

The Gooderhams treasured sailing skills as family heirlooms to be handed down at the helm. As he learned how to shorten sail by his father's side, George Horace also absorbed other family attributes: leadership and responsibility. He was president or director of four securities and insurance companies, owned one of the first automobile agencies, pioneered permanent highway construction, headed the Toronto-Hamilton Highway Commission, and introduced many traffic laws that have survived to this day. He felt that his wealth carried an obligation for community service. First elected to the Canadian National Exhibition (CNE) Board in 1896, he became president and life director. In 1904, he chaired Toronto's first Board of Education. Torontonians elected him to the Ontario legislature in 1908, 1911, and 1914; he later declined an invitation to serve as

The Oriole II *epitomized elegant Victorian yachting. On Gooderham & Worts' waterfront at the foot of Parliament Street, shipwrights fashioned the shallow-draft, centreboard schooner. Pine-planked on oak frames, the yacht's long pine spars supported a massive sail area that kept the centre of gravity low and reinforced stability. Her main topsail peaked 102 feet above her yellow pine deck, and the tip of the bowsprit to the end of the main boom measured 131 feet.*

lieutenant-governor. When he died on December 22, 1942, George Horace was president of Ridley College, St. Catharines.

Wealth also allowed George Horace to pursue his leisure passion. His spoon-bowed *Vivia*, imported from England in 1894, was the forerunner of the dominant pre-war P boats. The RCYC rear-commodore collected trophies on the Lake Yacht Racing Association circuit and helped his father organize the syndicate that mounted the first Canada Cup Challenge in 1896.

For his first term as RCYC commodore, from 1900 to 1903, George Horace commissioned a new flagship from the *Oriole II*'s designer, Cary Smith. *Clorita* combined an unusual keel and centreboard compromise, won the Prince of Wales Cup in her first year, and was one of the first sailboats to install the newly available auxiliary power engines. She often anchored beside *Oriole II,* her black hull and red underbody mirroring the colours that her parent yacht had made famous, in a tableau that reflected the father-son relationship. His next yacht, *Vivia II,* was part of the vital 1920s and '30s RCYC R Class fleet.

While his uncle was progressing up the flag-officer ladder, another future sailing star fed into the family continuum. The young Norman R. Gooderham was finding his sea legs in his grandfather's *Oriole II* and practising navigation techniques on the lawn. By 1903, he was crewing in the Canada Cup contender *Strathcona*.

When his P Class *Patricia* captured the Richardson Cup for international supremacy in 1912, the *London Times* called him "the most skillful freshwater yachtsman in the world." After a 1919 win in another P Class boat, *Bernice,* Prince Edward, Prince of Wales, presented him with the Prince of Wales Cup (donated to the club 59 years earlier by Edward's grandfather, King Edward VII).

The Universal Rating Rule

The Seawanhaka Rule, one of the earliest rating rules used in North America, originally rated length and sail area, which are two large factors in a boat's speed. Eventually, girth measurements fed into the equation. The New York Yacht Club (NYYC) asked the best contemporary yacht designers to come up with a simpler rule. In 1903, they adopted the Universal Rule developed by marine architect Nathaniel Herreshoff to rate racing yachts for handicap or level-class racing in which no handicaps applied. Based on a formula of critical measurements, a yacht's rating indicated potential speed. Rating was expressed in feet. Herreshoff also wrote minimum construction standards, called "scantling rules," as part of the rule. The Universal Rule was used to rate the yachts racing in the America's Cup Challenge.

Letters of the alphabet defined the classes. Classes A through G were for schooners, classes H through T for sloops and yawls. J Class boats were most famous; the R and Q Class boats most numerous. The upper limit for boats in classes H through T—mostly sloops—were:

H: Not over 100-foot rating
I: Not over 88 feet
J: Not over 76 feet
K: Not over 65 feet
L: Not over 55 feet
M: Not over 46 feet
N: Not over 38 feet
P: Not over 31 feet
Q: Not over 25 feet
R: Not over 20 feet
S: Not over 17 feet
T: Not over 15 feet

The formulae for the rule appear in early editions of Skene's *Elements of Yacht Design* (Dodd Mead).

The Oriole Logbook

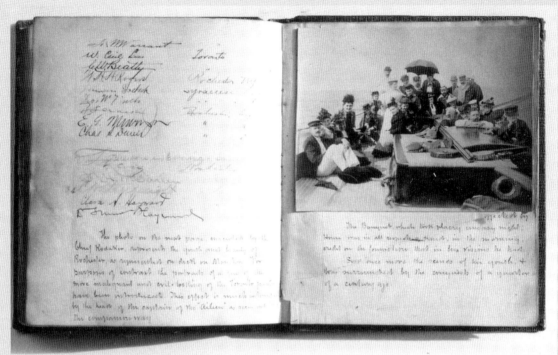

"The Afterguard." During this era when women usually stayed on shore, the Gooderhams often invited the "fair sex" on board. Notwithstanding, during official functions like sailpasts, the ladies were ushered below decks.

Unlike today's terse, technical log entries, the four elegant leather-bound *Oriole II* logbooks document Victorian society in flowing script and whimsical sketches. These volumes probably escaped winter mildew by being cloistered behind glass-windowed bookshelves in the library of George Gooderham's stone-and-brick mansion at the corner of George and Florence Streets, which now houses the York Club. The log entries tell of "rakish billowed sails" and summer regattas, entertainment, and fair guests hailing from far-flung ports. Some are reminiscent of American philosopher Henry David Thoreau's *Walden* musings or Lewis Carroll's whimsy.

Date unknown. Four am when abreast of Whitby lighthouse, the welcome sound of eight bells ended the labours of the port watch, or rather, should have done. There remained, however, the arduous task of getting the starboard watch on deck, and worse still, making them understand where they were and what was required of them. The application of cold water to the respective heads of the watch was recommended by the Doctor, and proved effective, but produced such a cloud of steam that the lighthouse keeper mistook it for a bank of fog, and immediately set his horn in vigorous operation.

Date unknown. The western pier was now thronged with pedestrians, mostly of the gentler sex, and the doctor, thinking no doubt that his services might be required, desired at once to go ashore. The professor accompanied him, ostensibly for the purpose of seeing Mars from a more favourable standpoint.

July 11th. The harbour this morning looked exceedingly beautiful. Some thirty yachts were at their moorings, their mainsails and topsails glistening white in the sun, which shone with tropical brightness on water that reflected the cloudless sky above. Scarcely a breath of wind was stirring, though outside, a light breeze filled the upper canvases of Charlotte and Mr. Vardy of Toronto, which lazily rounded the lighthouse. This was the day appointed for the smaller craft, but anything like racing seemed impossible. A deputation went in the morning to the summer residence of Mr. Crowther to request this gentleman to ascertain whether any of the Cobourg ladies would do us the honour of a sail in the afternoon.

July 12th. Regatta day but not regatta weather. Scarcely an air in the morning, later on a few cat's paws freshening to a soldier's breeze ... I think it's clearing up to windward, shouted the lawyer from his shelter behind the foremast where he was endeavouring to preserve in a dry and pristine condition his immaculate knickerbocker toggery as he leans over to sponge off the cabin skylights and raise them ...

Date unknown. Of the flirtations which took place, it behove the historian not to tell. How the One and Only George "sported from flower to flower." How the Doctor proved faithless to his Viennese memories. How the Ship's Uncle forgot his years and even the Professor, who had carefully secreted his spectacles and brushed the few surviving hairs over his dome, had thought to play the ancient beau. The evening garden party at Mrs. Crowther's formed a very appropriate ending to the day. The charming hostess, the entertainment and the delightful grounds with their lakeside walks ...

Date unknown. By two o' clock, there had assembled on board one of the fairest parties that has ever graced a dock. Even the frigid heart of old Boreus was warmed by the presence of such beauty. He thought of his youthful days when he lost his heart to the prettiest. The ancient god was propitiated and sent a gentle wind from his icy caves which bore us southward with our precious burden.

Date unknown. I have always found, said the skipper, who with the banker was chatting under the lee of the inclined mainsail, that when a man has made up his mind that a certain course is right, and it is his interest to pursue it, he should go right ahead, worry about nothing, trust to provi-

dence, keep his powder dry. And he will come out alright." In that case, said Mr. Mathemetician [sic], it is evidently time for a cocktail ... the libation was poured forth, dinner followed, and after a smoke, the Niagara Light was sighted, and at 9:15 the yacht came into safe moorings alongside the dock.

"Time for a horn," says the cheery voice of the Ship's Uncle as up through the companionway, the Saturday night toast of "sweethearts to wives" is lovingly drunk and the day is done.

July 15th. The harbour presented quite a deserted appearance, as most of the yachts had left during the night. At 10:20, bidding goodbye with regret to our friends, many of whom waved a farewell from the end of the pier, much discussion as to the course to be steered. The Only George, who had extended his fishing tackle, insisted that we should go through the Murray Canal, at the mouth of which there was said to be excellent sport. The ship was headed east southeast. After some time, the Doctor, whom we suspected of another appointment with the Viennese, suddenly remembered that he had another patient at Cobourg, and it was imperative that he should see to his welfare. We thereupon were headed up to east by north to please him. This was no sooner done than Captain Dick announced that we had no milk on board, and he must procure a supply from the lighthouse keeper's daughter, who kept cows. The yacht was accordingly to be put east to half south when the V.C. protested that for reasons best known to himself, he was determined to sleep at MacDonald's Cove that night. A vote being taken, the V.C. was supported and a course of east by south past south finally decided upon.

In her owner's absence, the Gooderham clan united to see to the Oriole's well-being. A lyrical log entry on July 29, 1892, starts with the signatures of George Horace

Gooderham, A. Gooderham, V. Gooderham, and W. Gooderham.

On the first day of a journey or cruise, the traveller's always more or less excitement of departure is succeeded by a point of reaction, which is typified by the influence of surroundings which are new and strange. Joking is out of the question. Stories are untold, nor could they secure a listener. Even conversation of the more desultory kind is irksome. With the soothing comes the feeling of contentment and repose. Nature unfolds, and gently charms. In the west, the sinking sun has left behind him a golden haze glinting the darkening outlines of the spires of chimneys of the receding city, while the electric lights like a circlet of diamonds sparkle and gleam in the gathering shadows beneath. The soft land breeze fills the yielding topsails, though the water below seems as glass, undisturbed save by the ripple of purple and gold which falls away in the wake. Silently we steal past the projecting headlands of the north water ... in the blackening sky the stars peek forth as the night closes over us.

A cruise on August 6, 1896, records: ... the wind rattled and creaked up their stays, and at 5:25 p.m. the starting gun boomed through the misty air. This swishing water rolled from our lee bow as the yachts gently careened under the easterly breeze, and quietly took our way to the eastern channel and thence on to Niagara. The Professor standing at the wheel in place of one of the sailing masters in oilskin coat, which was twice rolled around his body, and neatly buttoned down the back, presented a most interesting appearance, resembling more than anything else a newly dis-encoffined mummy wrapped in a shining asphalt.

To replace the *Oriole II,* which was broken up in 1906 following his father's death, Commodore Gooderham bought his new flagship, *Oriole III,* in New York. He sailed her through the Gulf of St. Lawrence to the Royal Canadian Yacht Club in June 1909. The American firm Townsend Downey built the three-masted schooner in 1904 from the plans of Cary Smith, who had designed her predecessors. She measured 113 feet LOA (length overall) and 89 feet LWL (length water line); her beam was 21 feet 4 inches, and her draft was 5 feet 10 inches. She was slow to windward, but combined with her shallow draft, her 6,000 square feet of sail gave her great speed off the wind. "She was a perfect witch at reaching, but she was seldom raced on Lake Ontario, although she accompanied the racing fleet on many occasions," reported the *RCYC Annals.* In a fast reach from Burlington to Toronto, she hit 16 knots, covering the 29 miles in 1 hour and 50 minutes.

George Horace Gooderham sold the *Oriole III* to a New Yorker. "He said he wouldn't sell her, but the man kept on pestering him for a price. Father set a price so high that he thought no one would buy it. And the man paid," remembers Gooderham's daughter, Mary Hogarth. "She was sold with everything on her. It had been initialled. Mother had done it all by hand, all the crystal, all the silver." R. S. McLaughlin brought her back to Toronto and restored her original name, *Azara.*

In March 1925, George Horace was elected RCYC commodore for his final term. In his final year, 1930, he helped found the Canadian Yachting Association. The Gooderham family had owned more yachts than anyone who had ever sailed on Lake Ontario. George Horace wanted to develop sailing as a sport that most families could enjoy. He started by organizing regattas in front of the CNE fairgrounds, where people could watch. To provide first-rate competition, he bought two previous

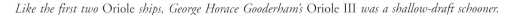

Like the first two Oriole *ships, George Horace Gooderham's* Oriole III *was a shallow-draft schooner.*

The visit of His Royal Highness Edward, Prince of Wales, highlighted the sailing season of 1919. On August 25, the RCYC fleet rode at anchor, ceremonial flags snapping briskly, as the steamer Hiawatha *deposited "the smiling prince" at the club's Island grounds. In 1900,* Hiawatha *skipper Captain David Reynolds had taxied the prince's father, King George V, then Duke of York, to the Island in the same launch. A huge marquee sheltered a gala garden party on the lawn. That evening, Commodore G. H. Gooderham hosted a reception on board his flagship, the three-masted schooner* Oriole III. *Daughter Mary was not allowed to attend, because she had not yet made her debut.*

Canada Cup champions, *Canada* and *Invader*, which Aemilius Jarvis had skippered to victory over Detroit's *Cadillac* in 1901.

Ever alert to spot and act on leading-edge design trends, George Horace picked up on the shifts that would replace the Universal Rule R and P boats as the dominant racing classes. The sailing world was now focussing on yachts that were designed to a different set of measurements, the sleek high-performance Metre boats. Gooderham imported the 1927 Scandinavian Gold Cup winner, the 6-Metre *Merenneito*. His clubmates were so impressed with her performance that they challenged the Rochester Yacht Club, the custodians of the Canada Cup, to defend this trophy in the 8-Metre Class. Accordingly, the RCYC designated Norman Gooderham to skipper *Quest*. While the challenging Canadians didn't win the series, the outcome was undecided until the last ten minutes of the final race

≈≈≈

"The key words would be initiative and enterprise, because whatever the Gooderhams turned their attention to, things were going to change!" So spoke RCYC Honorary Historian George Cuthbertson at the RCYC's 1991 Heritage Night. Speaking at this event, George Horace's daughter, Mary Hogarth, recalled childhood summers spent on the Toronto Islands. The family cottages on Centre Island were all named for her father's different yachts: the original was *Oriole III;* hers was *Oriole IV.* From the veranda, they could watch sailboats race on Toronto Bay. Mary had her own little sea boat, but the children were not allowed in *Oriole* until they could swim around it.

"Dad was a keen racer, but he was often seasick. To avoid the rough stretch of water, we took the train from Toronto to Belleville. At Kingston, Father would bring the cannon on deck. I always wanted to hold

my ears, but I wasn't allowed, as it was not the thing to do. We never cruised for longer than two weeks, because Father always had to get back for business. We kept a boat in the davits for a fishing tender. We always went to Cressy, where there were beautiful perch. The first thing, Dad would get Mother some perch, and then go off bass fishing. The *Oriole III* had a steward, captain,

Both on and off the water, George Horace Gooderham's dynamic vision and leadership personified the Gooderham family motto, toujours en avant *(always forward).*

mate, and engineer. The steward married the parlour maid. He cooked the most gorgeous spring onions I have ever tasted in my life. The *Oriole IV* had no steward or engineer. Of my brothers, Dean never sailed, but Henry did."

Over six decades, Gooderham leadership had guided RCYC flag officers and committees. Norman R. Gooderham's service spanned 37 consecutive years, including four as commodore. Norman's son, Bill, was the fourth generation of outstanding sailors involved in junior sailing. In 1935, he captained the junior sailing team and sailed in his father's schooner *Yolanda* with his sisters, Audrey and Ruth. Bill built a twelve-foot dinghy for himself and his sister Ruth, steaming the frames in the garage workshop. Ruth, the RCYC ladies' champion, was also the club's first junior girls' instructor.

In 1949, Bill Gooderham and his young bride, JoAnne, combined their honeymoon with an International 14 regatta in Bermuda, where they placed fourth. Superb helmsmanship and tactical skills qualified Bill Gooderham for two Olympics: the 1948 Star Class at Torquay, England, and the 1952 6-Metre Class in Helsinki, Finland. At home, he promoted the family-oriented Albacore Dinghy Class across Canada. Over a seven-year term as the Ontario Sailing Association's technical director, Bill Gooderham developed the OSA team, the Ontario Finn team, youth championships, provincial competitions, and teaching programs.

In the 1950s, Bill Gooderham dominated the 6-Metre Class. He skippered *Buzzy II* and *Buzzy III* to the *Globe and Mail* North American, the Canadian-American Team Racing, and the North American titles. He also defeated the top American boat, *Goose*, returning the Seawanhaka Trophy to Canada for the first time in 51 years. During a 1955 regatta, the wind died, casting the fleet adrift on Bellingham Bay. As her crew sang "Onward Christian Soldiers," a zephyr stirred *Buzzy II's* sails. She ghosted away from her stalled competition to give Gooderham his fourth consecutive North American Championship.

GOODERHAM IS SPORT ROYALTY, headlined a *Globe and Mail* story on December 29, 1979. "Canada's sailing community has lost a legendary member with the recent death of Norman William 'Bill' Gooderham."

The dynasty continues. Bill Gooderham's son, Bryan, won the 1990 World 8-Metre Championship in Rochester, New York, and successfully defended it the following year in Port Credit, Ontario. Bill's grandchildren, Yolande and Billy Gooderham and Will and Sarah Gyles, race dinghies on the junior circuit. Their forebears would approve.

The Forgotten Great Designer

Aflurry of yachting activity closed the nineteenth century. Joshua Slocum rebuilt an oyster smack called *Spray* and sailed into the record books with a single-handed circumnavigation of the world. Three hundred thousand entries flooded a contest to name the new America's Cup defender, designed by the great naval architect Nathaniel G. Herreshoff. Into this effervescent scene, a young naval architect named George Owen made his professional debut.

Kurt Hasselbalch, curator of the Hart Nautical Collection at the Massachusetts Institute of Technology (MIT), calls him "the forgotten great designer" of this era. Owen graduated from MIT in 1894 with a mechanical engineering degree. He also took courses from Professor Cecil H. Peabody, who established MIT's naval-architecture department the next year.

Overshadowed by his first employer, the illustrious Herreshoff, the young graduate moved to Hamilton, Ontario, in 1901 and joined several sailing clubs. During his brief Canadian residence, Owen acquired loyal clients who engaged him after he returned to New England. One man impressed by the young American was George Horace Gooderham. Owen-designed yachts soon dominated their classes at Marblehead, Narragansett Bay, Long Island Sound, and Great Lakes regattas, beating competition from

the drawing boards of better-known architects like Herreshoff, William Gardner, C. D. Mower, B. B. Crowninshield, and Sherman Hoyt. Owen's *Mavoreen* established a Mackinac Race record that stood from 1912 to 1926.

British tea merchant Sir Thomas Lipton issued five America's Cup challenges between 1899 and 1930. In response to his 1913 challenge to the New York Yacht Club (NYYC), three syndicates built boats for a sail-off to determine the American defender. NYYC flag officers J. P. Morgan and Cornelius Vanderbilt engaged Herreshoff. A second group retained Gardner to design *Vanitie*. The fourteen members of the third group, a consortium led by NYYC merchant banker George Mallory Pynchon and Boston's F. E. Peabody, chipped in $10,000 each to hire George Owen.

Owen's pedigree was, by then, well established, especially through a design that *Yachting* magazine deemed 1908's "Boat of the Year." When skippered by her designer, the N Class sloop *Dorello* was almost unbeatable, winning 58 of 68 races. She featured an innovative "high-aspect ratio rig," with the foresail set from the stem-head instead of the bowsprit. *The History of the NYYC* cites this rig as the chief technical reason for her success, along with her "near-perfect" hull form and her designer's

The Oriole IV*'s original sail area was 3,351 square feet. In 1924, area totalled 3,216 square feet, and in 1928 it was 3,277 square feet. Circa 1927.*

helming skills. Unlike the *Oriole II*'s long main boom, *Dorello*'s boom was drastically shorter than the mast, which placed the sail area high and inboard, where it was easier to manage. *Defiance,* the yacht Owen designed for the 1913 America's Cup defender sail-off, lost to Herreshoff's *Resolute*—many claimed it was because Owen was not at her helm.

By 1914, public interest in high-performance boats was rivalling New England's fascination with basketball. Large newspapers hired yachting editors to dutifully record the dramatic details of every race and profile the skippers. Along the Atlantic coast, yacht races drew a spectator gallery, especially at harbour-entrance start and finish lines. George Owen returned to MIT to teach naval architecture in 1915. Soon after, he began incorporating the *Defiance* bow and *Dorello*'s high-aspect rig into a yacht that would define and transcend her era: *Oriole IV.*

George Owen laid down the first lines for *Oriole IV*—moment and sheer curves, general arrangement, and section—in 1918, for his friend and mentor George Horace Gooderham of 49 Wellington Street East, Toronto, president of Northrop Strong Securities Ltd.

At the time Gooderham commissioned his new ketch, sailors were experimenting with a radical sail plan that used triangular instead of four-sided sails. This novel Bermuda rig was sometimes called the Marconi rig, because its long, tapering spars resembled the antenna for Guglielmo Marconi's newfangled invention, radio. P-boat sailors debated whether to adopt it for their class, and compromised by using it only in Cup competition. When Gooderham adopted the Marconi rig for his new flagship, his clubmates quickly followed. In 1921, the Owen-designed R boat *Scrapper* led the conversion to the new rig for that class.

Construction of what was to be the largest Great Lakes yacht from George Owen's drawing board started at the Toronto Dominion Shipbuilding Company, but labour problems closed the yard permanently. The boat's steel plates were loaded onto a train for Boston, but post-war chaos still haunted the railways, and the shipment never arrived. In Neponset, Massachusetts, George Lawley's yard unrolled the blueprints and started again. The profits of prohibition undoubtedly helped Gooderham pay the bills, which totalled $100,000 by the time *Oriole IV* was ready to launch.

On June 4, 1921, Gooderham's youngest daughter, Mary, christened the majestic new RCYC flagship. Her dad gave her a big bouquet of roses. Her mother brought a bottle of champagne from Canada, done up in ribbons of yellow and red, sewn together so no glass could fly. "I was so scared I couldn't crack it properly," she recalled many years later. "Of course it splashed, and the roses were dripping. It was prohibition, and all the men came rushing to lick the roses. She was christened truly and properly, no doubt about that."

Commodore Gooderham cruised back to Toronto at a leisurely pace after exiting the Gulf of Maine. He stopped at Halifax and along the Gaspé Peninsula and St. Lawrence River to show off the handsome new rigging advance. At home in Toronto Bay, RCYC juniors nicknamed the ketch "Mrs. O'Reilly." The commodore saw to it that his new pride and joy was well tended. As she rode out winter storms at her anchorage, a straw and manure moat protected her hull from steel-crushing ice.

Over the years, Owen drafted 50 more plans for modifications. In 1922, after the mainsail headboard had pulled out during a race, *Oriole*'s mainmast was shortened to 86 feet and the centreboard was removed. In 1924, a topmast was added and a new sail plan designed. In 1927, she acquired port-side davits, a bowsprit, and a double-headstay rig. A 1928 refit added a jib boom, and the mizzenmast was lengthened to 55 feet.

In 1932, Gooderham wrote to Owen and ordered a "very simple contrivance" for *Oriole*'s mainmast. Addressed to Professor George Owen at Cambridge's MIT, the July 19 letter is MIT's only record of correspondence between the pair. Gooderham's letter closes, "I trust that you will see that the price is as low as possible, as we have a difference in exchange and then a very high duty figured on the American price."

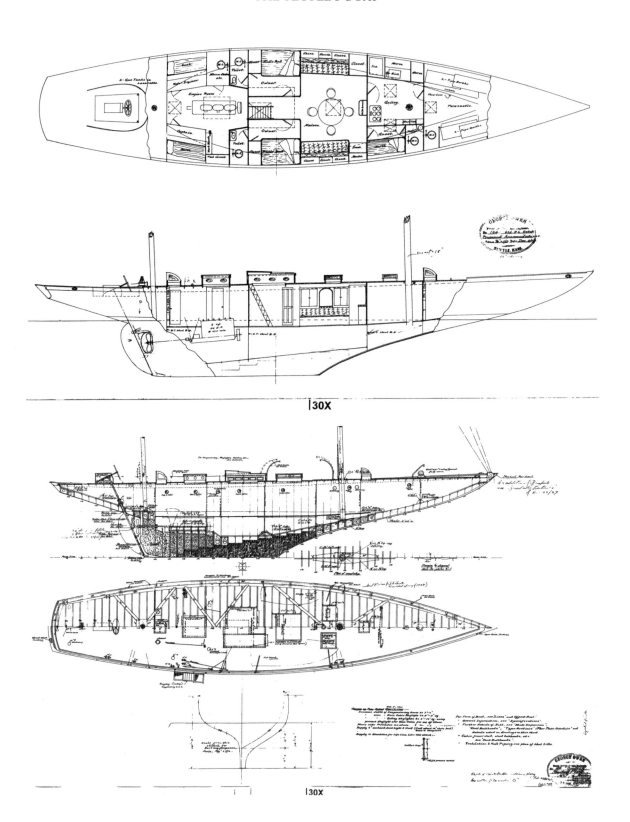

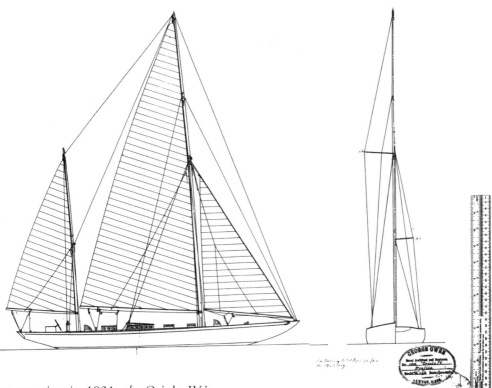

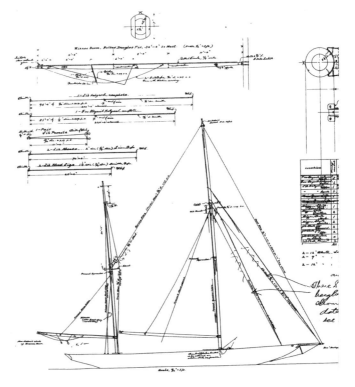

For construction in 1921, the Oriole IV's dimensions were 91 feet overall length, 60 feet waterline length, 19-foot beam, 9-foot draft, displacement 75 tons. The mainmast was 105 feet, the mizzenmast, 55 feet. She had steel frames, steel bulkheads, and a steel hull. Her decks, cleats, blocks, and hatch covers were teak.

For all his fascination with trend-setting technology, comfortable family cruising was a priority for Commodore Gooderham. The Oriole IV's accommodations had five "w.c.'s" (toilets) and three sinks. Crew sleeping quarters in the bow had four pipe berths. The galley and a guest berth squeezed into the space between the focs'le and the main salon, which featured a round dining table, fireplace, settees, closets, desk, and china cabinet. Two owner staterooms on either side of the companionway boasted a double bed, w.c., bathtub, and sink.

The Gooderham link to RCYC heritage remains in good hands today, in the person of Enid Maclachlan, wife of Peter Maclachlan. Peter was the son of George Horace Gooderham's daughter, Jessie, and K. S. Maclachlan, who saw active service in charge of Canadian Combined operations and was Admiral Troubridge's flag officer. Peter graduated in the first class at Victoria's Royal Roads Naval College and joined the Royal Navy as a midshipman. Peter and Enid met in wartime Britain, when Enid was a WREN photographer on assignment to HMS *Excellent*. Enid had earned her degree at London's Ealing School of Art, and when the couple came back to Canada, she taught art. She became a trustee of the Art Gallery of Ontario and chaired the City of Toronto's art commission.

In the RCYC city clubhouse, Enid organized displays of historical artifacts on the mezzanine level and in the model room. Illuminated by a large, south-facing corner window, the model-room walls showcase half-models of boats owned by members over the years. One of their most devoted guardians has been George Cuthbertson, Canada's foremost yacht designer for more than half a century. In 1969, he merged his company with three Ontario boat builders to form Cuthbertson and Cassian (C & C) Yachts, one of Canada's most successful yachting businesses.

Cuthbertson and Enid Maclachlan grouped the half-models into panels: specific eras that trace the evolution of design, and classes, like the R Class boats that dominated racing on Lake Ontario after the Great War.

Cuthbertson ranks George Owen "in the top echelon" of yacht designers. Starting with *Whirl* in 1902, RCYC half-models trace the evolution of the hulls that culminated in his masterpiece, *Oriole IV*. Several Owen designs drove the fleet of P Class yachts that dominated RCYC racing action until the Second World War. Norman R. Gooderham headed the syndicate that built the 51-foot *Patricia*, named for the daughter of the Duke and Duchess of Connaught. Between 1911 and 1939, *Patricia* collected 34 trophies, including the Prince of Wales, Mackinac, Richardson, and Fisher Cups. As an alternative to the large First Division yachts, the P-boat's two-piece sail plan averaged 1,000 square feet less than the older cutters, making it much easier for a six-man racing crew to handle.

Because club competition focussed on the R and P boats designed to the Universal Rule, the *Oriole IV* did not see much racing action. Commodore Gooderham had outfitted her lavishly for comfortable family cruising, and she fulfilled this role for two decades until her owner's declining health and the political climate across the Atlantic Ocean caused a dramatic shift in her fortunes.

Oriole's *spinnaker was "bird-less" until Bill Walker's captaincy, when one of the sailors drew the image using the ship's oriole logo.*

Top: Chris Johnson, Royal Vancouver Yacht Club Vic-Maui Race Committee member Paddy Thomson, and skipper Scott Crawshaw during a pre-race daysail. Bottom left and right: Before the race to Maui, boats and people crowd the Victoria Harbour finger floats in front of the Empress Hotel.

Above: The Oriole *crew before the start of the 2000 Vic-Maui race. Below: Dan Sinclair's* Renegade *crew, wearing pre-race "tropical khaki," in Victoria's Inner Harbour. Right:* Night Runner *is skippered by Seattle's Doug Fryer, who twice won Vic-Maui line honours.*

Top: HMCS Oriole *in the 2000 Vic-Maui Race. Bottom:* Oriole's *"victory run" along the Victoria waterfront upon her return from Maui.*

Oriole II *log images show burgee and royal plumage, which were important emblems from the Royal Canadian Yacht Club nineteenth-century racing era.*

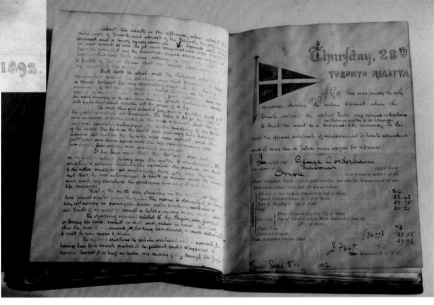

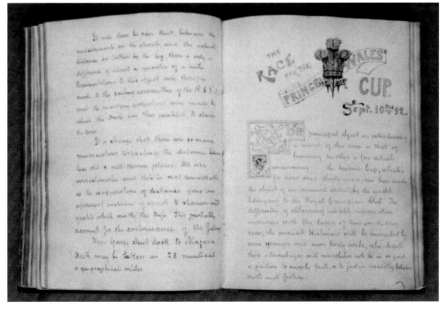

APPROVED

CHIEF OF NAVAL STAFF

OTTAWA ___ Oct 5ᵗʰ 19⁵²

MINISTER OF NATIONAL DEFENCE

OTTAWA ___ Oct 13 19 52

Left: The HMCS Oriole *crest took its place among the ships of the Royal Canadian Navy fleet in 1952. Below:* Oriole *iced up during a January return from Seattle in the mid-1970s.*

Above: HMCS Oriole *punches into an Atlantic storm on the way to OSQAR 84. Below right: Bow lookout on the way to OSQAR. Below left: Lookouts watch a slow 1999 Swiftsure start from* Oriole's *bowsprit.*

Above: Washington State's Mount Baker is the backdrop as HMCS Oriole *drives through turbulence in Baynes Channel between Victoria's Chatham Island and Ten Mile Point. Below: HMCS* Oriole, *destroyers* Yukon *and* Mackenzie *(shown here), and the minesweepers comprised the Fourth Squadron. Training sessions alternated between the classroom and the ships. In 1991, two destroyers were "keeping station" on* Oriole, *ranked as the senior ship because the squadron commander, Captain Brown, was on board.*

IN THE PUBLIC DOMAIN

Called for Icing

*A*fter a twenty-year idyll in the private sector, *Oriole IV* entered the public domain. By the beginning of the Second World War, George Horace Gooderham was confined to a wheelchair. For several years, he had loaned *Oriole IV* to the Navy League of Canada, a volunteer community organization that provides marine-oriented training for young Canadians. The year before he died, he sold *Oriole IV* to a friend, Gordon Leitch, who was president of Toronto's Upper Lakes and St. Lawrence Transportation Co. Ltd. of Queen's Quay. Two days later, on May 1, 1941, the firm resold her to the Navy League. The League retained the yacht's five professional crew and paid their wages. With brass polished and dress flags flapping, *Oriole IV* idled in the sunshine hard by the training ship *Pathfinder* and the Norwegian steamer *Iris*. Leitch joined fellow Navy League officials and Royal Canadian Naval Volunteer Reserve (RCNVR) officers to celebrate this landmark change of command.

That same year, the navy assumed its first official role in sea cadet affairs. Toronto Naval Reserve Division HMCS York supplied uniforms, instructors, and training facilities. Beausoleil, the League-sponsored cadet camp on Georgian Bay, accepted *Oriole*'s first summer students. Peaked caps with a white anchor badge and the letters GCC identified the Grove Cadet Corps from Lakefield Preparatory School (now Lakefield College School), north of Peterborough. They slept ashore in hammocks and wore officer-type uniforms with rows of brass buttons down the jacket front.

Lakefield Preparatory School Grove cadets execute sailing manoeuvres following International Code signals flown from a mast on shore.

In June 2001, 60 years after first boarding *Oriole IV,* a graduate of that first sea cadet class went sailing in HMCS *Oriole* during Victoria's world military regatta. Robert Webster remembers his cadet instructor, Royal Navy Chief Petty Officer George Lee, who had been decorated in the First World War for sinking a German submarine. "He fired up a lot of us boys to be interested in the navy. I left sea cadets and went on active service as an ordinary seaman, served in the North Atlantic in the corvette HMCS *Fredericton*, then was drafted to HMCS *Haida*. I stayed on in the reserves after the war and served in various ships, from minesweepers to an aircraft carrier. I retired as a lieutenant. No matter where I went in the navy, in Canada or overseas, I met men I had known in the Grove Cadet Corps."

During the Second World War, Lieutenant Peter Pangman saw active duty with British and Canadian naval forces in the Far East and on D-day. Bill Gooderham sat on the 1947 Navy League committee that appointed the young veteran, who had previously taught sailing to RCYC juniors, as summer skipper for the Royal Canadian Navy Sea Cadet Ship (RCNSCS) *Oriole*. Pangman recruited two ex-navy men as bosun and chief engineer. The engineer, a friend of Pangman's from the University of Toronto, doubled as cook.

Dressed in white middy top, long pants, and running shoes, each cadet took a turn on the wheel and navigated with compass, charts, and dead reckoning. Pangman enforced strict discipline, allowed no gambling or alcohol, and restricted smoking to the upper deck forward of the companionway on watch or during "stand easy" breaks.

The new program attracted widespread newspaper coverage. The sight of the stately yacht nodding at Kingston Causeway caused minor traffic jams. Pangman's bride, Eve, often went along on training cruises. A Toronto paper noted, "She was a valuable extra hand in times of crises, mixing with local dignitaries, and by her presence curbed much

of the sailor-like language the cadets were inclined to adopt."

In 1948, RCNSCS *Oriole*'s summer schedule resembled a debutante's datebook during coming-out season. Over 61 days, the ketch travelled 1,750 miles—some 1,500 under power; entertained 117 committees and dignitaries; trained 622 cadets and officers from 24 Ontario sea cadet corps; and visited 17 lakeside ports.

Pangman's log entries enthuse that she was "glorious in a breeze. She would drive through and flatten the waves, so that we had little green water to

Behind an unidentified officer at left and RCNSCS Oriole*'s summer skipper Peter Pangman (right), port davits suspend the narrow wooden ship's tender. The RCYC newsletter* Kwasind *carried Pangman's race account: "We started in light air from the southwest but it hauled through north into a severe northeaster. Oriole started to 'chomp.' At about 3:00 a.m. as we tacked for our final approach to Stoney our mizzen halyard parted and within seconds the top 30 feet of the mainmast and upper rigging collapsed on our lifeboat which was on the portside davits. Unable to lift the wreckage due to its weight, the seas and our high freeboard we managed to lash her close to avoid full damage. Several attempts to start the engine failed so we fired distress rockets. The US Coast Guard arrived at dawn and towed us into Sackett's Harbour from where we powered home."*

Casey Baldwin's dog Six-O poses with the crew that delivered Oriole IV *to Halifax from Toronto. Front, left to right: W. R. Wood, R. M. Steeves, Sydney Simmons, C. S. Sackfield, Warren Brown. Rear: D. H. Delisle, Kenton R. Sutherland, T. B. Anderson, Lieutenant John Agnew, Lieutenant P. A. Baldwin, Lieutenant Herman Baker, Lieutenant J. M. Cutts, Chief Petty Officer Raymond A. Moore, L. H. Lafond, Donald W. Murphy, and Howard W. Glover.*

worry about." To keep the cadets interested, *Oriole* sometimes raced. Clubs around Lake Ontario held many international regattas. Pangman's September 1948 report warned of increased competition for teen leisure hours and concluded that sea cadet programs should be made more attractive. To raise their profile, he suggested a public-relations person be employed. And to provide more excitement, he recommended a more active racing program. "I find the cadets far keener on a trip that had some objective in a new port rather than just going out for a one day's sail. The light August winds hold no promise for the 16-year-olds, but when there was a breeze, they just adored it. They loved the overnight sails, standing watch, the experience of seeing ships at night."

Pangman reckoned that with major conversions, *Oriole* could comfortably accommodate fifteen cadets on long cruises. The wardroom needed better table and seating arrangements. The owner's staterooms, which still had their original bed, sink, and bathtub, needed restructuring. But, as Pangman had predicted, teenagers lost interest in cadet programs, so the Navy League offered to lend its yacht to the regular navy. In October 1949, the Naval Board approved the transfer, but ordered an inspection. Lloyds appraised *Oriole IV* at $14,500. She returned to armed forces service on November 18, 1949, for a charter fee of one dollar.

The next chapter in the *Oriole* saga started with a race against nature. That year, the ketch was the last boat to make it out of the Great Lakes before the winter freeze-up shut down the St. Lawrence River lock system. The navy had less than a week between charter and departure to cobble together a crew that knew how to sail and could overhaul her musty gear. Some experienced mariners responded to the call for volunteers. Her delivery skipper, Lieutenant Herman Baker, was a seasoned Newfoundland reservist. A dockyard bosun charged with moving ships for refit, he always kept wood shavings in his pocket to throw into the water to test the current. First Lieutenant John Agnew's father was the commanding officer at RMC Kingston.

Gordon Mills was a Queen's University Naval Training Division (UNTD) cadet. Like Robert Webster, he had learned to sail in Lakefield's Akroyd dinghies and continued in *Oriole* at Beausoleil summer camp. Mills arrived in Toronto to find his old ship rusting alongside Pier Six at the foot of Yonge Street. There was no money for gear or uniforms, so the new crewmen brought their own blue jeans and set to work. They scrounged parts and rebuilt the frail engine. They discovered her fragile sails rotting in a shed, spread them out, and patched them. There was no spinnaker.

Snow swirled on November 24, 1949, as the former RCYC flagship left Toronto for the last time to port-hop to Nova Scotia. At Kingston, the men took advantage of HMCS Cataraqui Naval Reserve Unit's waterfront facilities to thaw. Fog slowed their progress to Brockville, where the off-duty watch helped firemen fight a business-district blaze. The next day, a favourable current lifted *Oriole* eastward. At Lachine, ice froze her to the jetty overnight. The next day, she followed in the path cleared by a lake freighter bound for Montreal. At Quebec City, *Oriole* rendezvoused with training vessel HMCS *Portage*, her assigned escort. *Portage* cleared herself of ice, hauled her charge into open water, and took her in tow. After the line snapped, *Oriole* flashed up her engine, but at 5 knots, it was slow going.

In open water, another icy blast buffeted *Oriole*. For fourteen hours she ran under bare poles before a Gulf of St. Lawrence gale. Snow reduced visibility, and the two boats lost contact. When the wind veered northward off the Gaspé coast, *Oriole* hove to under a makeshift storm sail until *Portage* found her and took up the tow. Finally, the yacht reduced speed to 2 knots after her rigging and deck iced up. It took seventeen days for the exhausted crew and weather-worn *Oriole IV* to reach Halifax harbour.

Training cruises on Great Lakes, circa 1940s. Top: The executive officer for Oriole IV's *delivery to Halifax, Lieutenant P. A. "Casey" Baldwin (shown here at the wheel), was a superb seaman who always travelled with his black-and-white setter Six-O. Years earlier, in Baddeck, Nova Scotia, Casey's father, F. W. Baldwin, a keen racing sailor at the Royal Canadian Yacht Club, built an R Class yacht designed by* Bluenose *architect Wm. Roue. Like his friend Alexander Graham Bell, the senior Baldwin liked to tinker. Until he ran out of money, he experimented in the 1920s with a light, high-speed hydrofoil design that he hoped could be used by the navy. Bottom left:* Oriole IV *crew shares the foredeck with the ship's wooden dinghy during a summer sail on Lake Ontario. Bottom far right: The crew prepares a breakfast of freshly caught fish on the* Oriole IV *stern.*

The Nova Scotia Navy

*T*o cope with wartime manpower shortages, the seamanship training school HMCS Cornwallis opened in 1942 on the Bay of Fundy near Digby, Nova Scotia. At that time, Canada's navy consisted of six River Class destroyers and seven smaller ships. Cornwallis was closed after the war, but later recommissioned, graduating its first new-entry training class of 129 men on September 23, 1949.

The Naval Board transferred *Oriole IV* to this program in January 1950. Conversions had modified the yacht for her new training role. Her wardroom now housed the radio transmitter-receiver and chart case. Sixteen people could sit at two tables. Cabins for the captain and two watch officers flanked the companionway. Her remodelled stern housed an Ailsa Craig engine, generator, and two small cabins for the permanent stoker and three seamen.

Casey Baldwin was charged with organizing routines. Every Monday, a group of new-entry seamen boarded *Oriole* and sailed the next day for Grand Manan Island or Saint John, New Brunswick, returning on the Friday. That summer, another outstanding professional seaman skippered *Oriole* for the first time. Ellsworth T. "Tubby" Coggins had grown up among the Nova Scotia South Shore fishing schooners. His steam experience qualified him for the Royal Canadian Naval Reserve (RCNR) and

landed him a berth in the minesweeper HMCS *Gaspe* at the beginning of the war. By the time he took the helm of *Oriole*, Coggins had earned his coast master's papers and foreign-going mate's certificate.

After her summer stint at Cornwallis, *Oriole* was transferred to Halifax. The next year, extensive repairs reduced her sea time. With maintenance bills mounting, flag officers from both coasts met with the vice chief of naval staff in November 1951 to discuss her fate. They decided to lease *Oriole IV* for another year, invest in a winter refit, and place her under the administration of HMCS Stadacona Seamanship School.

The navy commissioned HMCS *Oriole* on June 19, 1952. She immediately left for St. Pierre and Miquelon, carrying the Nova Scotia-based French consul. Trainees in the Junior Officer Training and Leadership (JOTL) course helped Captain Coggins coax the ketch to a glorious 13.7-knot average over the 460-nm distance. The return voyage was not so joyful. *Oriole* broke her bowsprit and mizzenmast. Repairs consumed most of July.

In August, officer trainees from Halifax Naval Air Station HMCS Shearwater sailed *Oriole* to Cape Breton. Then she represented the navy at Lunenburg's annual fisheries exhibition. With winter approaching, her running rigging was removed, she

Whaler crews from HMCS Stadacona get a tow to HMCS Shearwater from Halifax Dockyard to take part in an August 1952 regatta. More than 75 boats participated, from the Royal Nova Scotia Yacht Squadron, Armdale Yacht Club, and navy ships and shore establishments.

was laid up with steam heat, and her upper deck was covered in canvas.

The next year, training programs enrolled leadership candidates and reserves at Stadacona, and naval airmen and ordinary seamen at Shearwater. Sea cadets came from across Canada to polish, scrub, and sail. One highlight of that third East Coast summer was a regatta in Massachusetts. *Oriole* visited various U.S. ports, including Gloucester, Massachusetts, Lunenburg's arch rival in the international fishing schooner races. At Manchester, she joined the sail-training sloop *Grilse* for a biennial race to Halifax.

Nature masterminded *Oriole's* next adventure. On a 1953 Halifax-to-Gloucester training cruise, the ship ran into bad weather offshore. As so often happens in this area, a late-summer wind came up off North Carolina's Cape Hatteras, curved off Nova Scotia, and spun out to sea, causing problems for ships in its path. It was a memorable experience for crew members. "We were caught literally in the middle of this hurricane going by," recalls James Butterfield, one of fifteen JOTL trainees.

While it was still daylight, the wind was making up. By dark, it was screaming. "We were running

Sea cadets "heave" on the sheet during a 1952 summer training session in Halifax.

under bare poles, trying to keep *Oriole* comfortable," says Butterfield. "You couldn't see or hear anything for the wind and the spray and the howling of the gale. Then suddenly there was absolute dead calm. Nothing. The wind totally died, while we went through the textbook centre of the system."

The *Oriole* wallowed among confused, oily seas, her mahogany-panelled wardroom awash. Coggins left the bridge to bail with his trainees in the wardroom. Knee-deep in water, they briskly heaved brimming buckets up the companionway. In an hour, the worst of the water was gone. Then, whammy! The storm filled in from the other quarter.

"A vessel like *Oriole* can sit out in pretty well any darn thing, but you still have to look after it," says Butterfield. He calls that 1953 training cruise "exhilarating." He explains, "For two weeks, we were taken out and rolled around on the big sailboat to show that engines didn't matter too much if the right vessel and the right people came together to

keep her afloat. The sea is a manual thing. It's not a touchy-feely, push-button type of thing, which is why *Oriole* is hugely important. In those days, weather wasn't something you worried about or tried to avoid. Weather was something you put up with and took appropriate action to deal with. So it wasn't a matter of there we were, purposely getting into a hurricane. We had a radio warning, but nothing like today. We knew we were in for bad weather, but the radio was not particularly good."

Walter Blandy was another JOTL trainee who joined the wartime navy through the volunteer stream. As a junior sailor, he had learned how to handle small boats at the Royal Victoria Yacht Club. He was nineteen when he enlisted in the RCNVR. After crash courses at Winnipeg Reserve Division HMCS Chippewa, and lectures at Dalhousie University, new recruits were posted to Halifax. Following a brief service in motor launches on the English Channel in the final months of the war,

Blandy returned to Canada. When the peacetime navy expanded, reserves were given a chance to join the permanent force. "The navy realized that we were lacking in formal training, so they organized a year's JOTL course based in Halifax to give us some of the basics we had missed," he recalls. "It was in-depth training, because up until then training had been very superficial."

To qualify as an officer in the post-war Canadian navy, even veterans like Blandy and Butterfield started as sub-lieutenants in the JOTL program, earning their sea time in *Oriole*. During Blandy's course, she travelled to the "gut" of Canso, between Cape Breton and the mainland, and back to Halifax. Blandy calls Captain Tubby Coggins "one hell of a good officer, and a damn good C/O of the *Oriole*.

He got things done, he didn't get too many backs up doing it, and he ran a tight ship, neat and clean. You knew where you stood with him."

The *Oriole* had three watch officers for the Canso cruise: Coggins, Training Officer Bob Welland, and Sub-Lieutenant Walter Blandy. "I was the only trainee picked for responsibility," says Blandy, "because I was the only one in the group who had any small-boat experience. I was offered the job of taking *Oriole* around to Victoria, but said, 'No thanks.' I was trying to get away from the yachting side into the tin-ship side of the navy, and get command of a destroyer some day. I didn't want the responsibility." By the time Commander Walter Blandy retired from the navy, he had captained several warships.

Crew members relax along the spars as Oriole IV *heads toward her berth at the Shearwater jetty.*

From Sea to Sea

*L*eif Stolee was first lieutenant in HMCS *Dauphine,* training sea cadets in Hamilton, Ontario, when a bulletin came asking for volunteers to deliver *Oriole* to Esquimalt, British Columbia. He arrived in Halifax to find the ship in dry dock, awash with riggers and carpenters. Caulkers pounded what looked like old rope into her deck seams and sealed them with tar. Mechanics tinkered with the new 160-horsepower engine. On July 19, 1954, she was recommissioned, and she spent the next two days motoring to the harbour mouth to adjust her compass and calibrate her direction finder (D/F). The ship's crew stored enough provisions to last until Bermuda.

With Lieutenant-Commander Ellsworth T. Coggins, RCN, at the helm, HMCS *Oriole* embarked on her first long saltwater voyage on a sunny July 23, 1954. Watch captains were Commander M. Smith, RCN (Reserve), Executive Officer, HMCS *Donnacona,* Montreal Reserve Division; Lieutenant E. J. Lattimer, RCN (Reserve), Montreal; and Lieutenant Leif Stolee, RCN (Reserve) of Edmonton. Her six petty officers, five leading seamen, and nine able seamen hailed from Saskatchewan, Ontario, Nova Scotia, Manitoba, Quebec, Newfoundland, and Alberta.

Barely out of port, the ship ran into a fog bank the likes of which prairie boy Stolee had never seen.

There was no radar, which unnerved the men, who could hear naval vessels on manoeuvres close by. The RCMP's *St. Roch,* bound for Vancouver's Maritime Museum, had left Halifax at the same time as *Oriole.* The Mounties had radar. If danger threatened, they were supposed to call the *Oriole* on her radio. But *Oriole*'s antiquated radio sputtered and died as she passed McNab Island near the mouth of Halifax harbour.

Stolee wrote in the navy magazine *Crowsnest,* "We had no fear, however, for we were well equipped to deal with navigational hazards: a D/F set, a radio, and an oversized hand-bellows foghorn. Four ships tried to run us down, but we eluded their clumsy efforts and straightway set course southward."

After several clammy days, the crew welcomed the Gulf Stream's warm sun. Leif Stolee knew how to read the wind. He had sailed all his life, first as a missionary's son in Madagascar, and later as a University Naval Training Division trainee, in cutters and whalers. He tells this story:

One afternoon when we were headed toward Bermuda, under full sail running just off the wind, the other lieutenant was standing proudly by the helmsman, all togged out in his best. I was lounging in my jeans on the deck—a perfect disgrace, in his eyes—and noticed that the wind was veering, and became worried. So I went up to him quietly and told him that he had better alter his course about ten degrees, as he might gybe and cause a bit of damage or, worse, carry away the mainmast. He looked down his nose at me and said, "The captain told me to run this course. I am the officer of the watch." I tried to explain that it didn't matter what the captain had said about the course. The wind was backing, and he was putting the boat in danger. He told me to buzz off, or words to that effect.

Luckily, the *Oriole* then had movable, or running, backstays to the mainmast. They were operated by long-handled levers that could be released by lifting or slammed down on deck to take up the strain. Since I did not want to go down to the captain's cabin—I assumed Tubby was having his afternoon nap—and tell him that the officer of the watch didn't have a clue about sailing, I went over and sat on the deck beside the starboard backstay and waited for the inevitable.

The wind gusted and backed suddenly, catching the main and mizzen on the wrong side. It overwhelmed the helm, and both boom and sails slammed over to port. As the main boom swung past amidships, I grabbed the lever and slammed down the backstay, thus giving the main mast the extra support it needed.

Tubby Coggins popped out of the hatch like a gopher chased by a garter snake, and immediately sized up what had happened. I don't know what he said to the dandy on watch, but I noticed he did not make that mistake again.

Southerly and southwesterly winds prevailed as *Oriole*'s bowsprit lifted and plunged toward the south. At one point, Stolee's watch thought they could see Bermuda's lights. When the grey dawn brought no sign, they were blamed "most harshly" for losing the first landfall. Leading Seaman (L.S.) Newton terrorized his shipmates with stories about the horrors of being lost at sea. Then he climbed the mast and sighted land.

On July 30, HMCS *Oriole* tied up in St. George's. This was no small feat, because the crew's only Bermuda harbour charts were for Hamilton. "We all fell on our knees," Stolee recalls. "The cook waved his meat chopper. L.S. Jones shouted, 'I name you Berma-do.'"

The crew bought a new radio with dials and buttons that spun automatically like a roulette wheel. The lads devised a game. They would place their money on the table, and L.S. Burchell would make a few magic passes and spin all the buttons. When the motion stopped, Burchell would scoop the money and call out, "Next." The new radio could pick up Hong Kong, Sydney racing results, New York boxing matches, and London symphony concerts. It could tune in almost everything except naval transmissions.

Coggins divided the crew into three watches, which soon acquired nicknames. Angel watch could do no wrong. Coconut watch was always in trouble. The White watch was renamed between Bermuda and Cuba, when they were trying to find Turk Island Passage. The lookout, perched on the crosstrees where the spreaders attach to the mast, bellowed, "Thar's the light!" The watch whooped and hollered as they stampeded to their tacking stations. With a banging of canvas, they brought the ship about. Below, the groggy sailors, bent on revenge, were tumbling out of their bunks when out of the blackness quavered a voice. "Ah, sahib, the elephants

The Gate vessel Porte de la Reine, *shown sliding down the Victoria Machinery Depot ways, was the first naval vessel launched in Victoria after the Second World War.*

have mustered." And thus the Elephant watch got its nickname.

On August 14, the Canadian sailors arrived at the American naval base in Cuba. Batista still held power, but Castro loomed in the Sierra Madre. Guantánamo City existed as a military rest-and-recreation suburb. Coggins' official report notes, "Leave in Guantánamo Bay was restricted to the U.S. Naval Base except for an excursion to Guantánamo City on August 16th, during which the mental health and physical safety of the ship's company were subjected to the recklessness of the local taxi-drivers."

A week later, *Oriole* anchored inside the Canal Zone breakwater and engaged a pilot for the trip in to the Coco Solo U.S. Naval Base. At the Panama Canal locks, the yacht tied up alongside a medium-sized freighter and hitched a timesaving ride. The next day, *Oriole* rendezvoused in Balboa with a Canadian navy auxiliary vessel sent to escort her back to Esquimalt. *Porte de la Reine* was designed to attach anti-submarine nets to drum buoys and string them across harbours. To the sailors cooped up in the spartan ketch, she looked like a floating palace. She was a Gate vessel (boats named after the Quebec Gates), and she had showers, hot water, and storage space. Her decks didn't leak. Everyone had a bunk. Water didn't slosh around the mess deck or get in the porridge on rough days. Her civilian crew enjoyed dry clothes, fresh food, radar, and a normal radio that was content to reach Esquimalt instead of Singapore.

Off Baja California, the two ships sheltered in the lee of Cedros Island, which was deserted except for a small abalone cannery and a few diving tenders. The next day, stiff headwinds ambushed them and forced a return to their anchorage. During a sultry, windless afternoon, a bright mass the size of a soccer ball appeared on the foremast and started to travel. Stolee took the wheel and sent the two seamen down the engine-room hatch. It made no sense to have all three men on deck, exposed to a wandering electrical flame. The sphere wandered hither and yon, crackling but causing no harm. Eventually it vanished. "When I told Coggins, he said it was St. Elmo's fire—which Lake Ontario sailors called 'Corpse Lights'—an electrical charge produced by certain storm conditions, and that he was not surprised because conditions were ideal," Stolee recalls. "We were lucky. The Patron Saint of Sailors was obviously just looking us over, having no harm in mind."

After a 73-day, 7,798-nm voyage from Halifax, HMCS Oriole *arrived in Esquimalt wearing her flying jib, jumbo jib, mainsail, and mizzen sail. Shrinkage on the thread that stitched the seam and bolt rope caused vertical creasing. Coggins' report summarized, "We sailed from Halifax with an inexperienced crew of volunteers, and by the time we reached Bermuda, we had shaken down completely, and had become an eager team of sailing enthusiasts. Out of the ship's company, only three had previous sailing experience in large sailing vessels. Despite the cramped and overcrowded accommodation space, the behaviour of the ship's company was excellent, and reflected the highest credit on the RCN in our ports of call. By the time we reached Esquimalt, the ship's company had become so efficient in handling sails that they could set all sails and lower and secure again in a matter of a few minutes."*

The boats made slow progress against the strong westerlies and northwesterlies. *Oriole* carved long tacks across her escort's stern. But the prevailing winds were now on her nose, so she often fired up her "iron genny," as sailors call the motor. While they were underway, her escort transferred fuel, water, and food to the *Oriole*. On September 9, the yacht passed medical supplies to the power vessel. Coggins wrote, "It should be noted that throughout the voyage from Balboa to Esquimalt, Petty Officer Threlfall carried out the medical duties aboard both ships in a most satisfactory manner."

In San Diego the crew cleaned, dried, painted, and stored. They inspected 8,500 square feet of Egyptian cotton sails: jumbo, main, mizzen, spinnaker, and genoa jib. Petty Officer King and Able Seaman Woods repaired the ragged foresails. Stolee and L.S. Newton made new canvas hatch covers to prevent water from cascading through the cracks whenever a large wave broke over the deck. The Kiwanis Club invited the officers from the *Porte de la Reine*, *Oriole*, and *St. Roch* to a luncheon.

Off the Santa Cruz Channel, the convoy ploughed through heavy swells. The ketch trailed the powerboats. Neither of them could slow down. The yacht could go no faster. For the first time, Stolee was apprehensive. Each wave that broke over the deck filled his sea boots with icy water. Every gust of wind and large wave stopped the ketch dead in the water. She would immediately pay off 30 to 40 degrees on either side before she picked up enough way to get her head back into the wind again. After they turned around and ran before the gale, the ship was as level as a pool table. Within two hours they hove to in the lee of Santa Cruz Island.

Westerly winds prevailed during the 513-nm passage to San Francisco. On September 25, *Oriole* tied up for the first of what would be many times at Treasure Island, the large U.S. Navy base. Stolee went to the opera and observed that everyone seemed to have an especially virtuous time. "It may have been the proximity of Alcatraz and San Quentin that had such a salutary effect on the lads."

North of San Francisco, *Oriole* could barely make headway against the large swells. "It is a strange feeling to see your bow raise up that high and to realize that you are sliding backwards down the waves with very little control from the helm," says Stolee. Coggins realized it was highly likely that the yacht would fall off, and possibly broach. Tucking in behind a headland, the captain dropped the pick in Drake's Bay and stayed put until the weather improved. "At that time of year along that coast, you simply cannot find shelter that readily," says Stolee, "so we stood well out to sea and sloughed our way north, and finally rounded Cape Flattery."

Lieutenant-Commander Coggins turned HMCS *Oriole* over to the HMCS Venture training program and took command of HMCS *Sault Ste. Marie*. After he left the navy, he became sail master in the *Bounty* replica built for the movie *Mutiny on the Bounty*. In 1963, he was hired to skipper the new *Bluenose II* replica. Forty-seven years later, retired educator Leif Stolee still sails British Columbia waters in chartered yachts.

Is-whoy-malth, "shoaling waters," as the First Nations peoples called Esquimalt, had one of the best harbours on the Pacific coast. Hudson's Bay Company factors considered its shores too rocky for a fort and trading post, so they built them at adjacent Camosack, now called Victoria. For Royal Navy (RN) purposes, however, Is-whoy-malth's narrow entrance between Duntze Head and Fort Rodd allowed easy access to a sheltered basin. The RN's Pacific Station stretched from Chile to Alaska, where skirmishes with Russian ships were common. To establish a permanent presence, in June 1885 Britain opened Esquimalt's Royal Naval Establishment. It was also an ideal base for fleet maintenance and storage facilities like Cole Island ammunition depot (top centre). Duntze Head is at left edge of photo, centre, and the Dockyard small boat jetty where HMCS Oriole *berths is behind Signal Hill, just off the right-hand edge of the photo.*

Shortly after her arrival from Halifax, HMCS Oriole *was dry-docked for repairs. In 1886, while stone cutters quarried huge granite blocks for the British Navy dry dock, Prime Minister Sir John A. Macdonald drove the last Esquimalt and Nanaimo Railway spike. By the new century, a cavernous brick ship-repair building replaced the naval station's wooden machine, blacksmith, and shipwright shops. Small brick houses and rectangular administration blocks fanned toward Duntze Head bluff and meandered up forested Signal Hill. Circa 1954/55.*

HMCS VENTURE YEARS

To Dare and Be Not Afraid

*H*MCS *Oriole*'s move to the West Coast marked a new beginning for her. Yet no one could have predicted that *Oriole*'s contribution at Esquimalt would still be significant 50 years later.

History repeated itself when HMCS *Oriole* came west to solve a recruiting crisis. Staffing shortfalls had brought another venerable vessel to Esquimalt four decades earlier, before the Great War. Until May 1910, when the Naval Service Act created the Royal Canadian Navy, Royal Navy ships patrolled Canadian waters.

HMS *Rainbow,* one of two light cruisers purchased from the British Admiralty, steamed into Esquimalt Harbour on November 8, 1910. The other, HMS *Niobe*, went to Halifax as *Rainbow*'s counterpart.

On November 9, the Crown formally transferred the Esquimalt naval base to Canada. This new national defence responsibility meant that Canada now had to recruit and train her own officers and men. *Rainbow* and *Oriole* are names forever tied to that enduring tradition.

With the navy's formation, the Royal Naval College of Canada was established at Halifax to train much-needed officers. Its history there was short— its classrooms were casualties in the 1917 explosion. The facility relocated briefly to Kingston, and then to Esquimalt. Anchored in the harbour, HMCS *Rainbow* billeted the displaced students.

With the Canadian navy coming into being shortly before the beginning of World War One, the co-existence of enlisted and volunteer navies was soon a reality. The idea for a "citizen navy" with volunteer units across the country came from HMS *Rainbow's* captain, Commander Walter Hose, who had trained Newfoundland fishermen for the Royal Naval Reserve. In 1913 he helped organize a group of Victoria citizens to offset the diminished permanent navy force. A 1914 order-in-council created the Royal Canadian Naval Volunteer Reserve (RCNVR). After war was declared on August 4, 6,000 reservists saw active war service.

The RNCVR was disbanded in 1920, but its traditions were succeeded by two entities: The Royal Canadian Naval Reserve (RCNR), which enrolled trained merchant mariners, and the Royal Canadian Naval Volunteer Reserve (RCNVR), which was nicknamed the "Wavy Navy." By April 1941, the RCNVR was supplying more than half of Canada's mobilized naval strength. After the war, the RCNR and RCNVR merged into one unit, the Royal Canadian Naval Reserve. Today, 4,000 men and women in 24 naval reserve divisions staff the Maritime Coastal Defence Vessels (MCDV).

Many nations still mount sail-training programs for their military, coast guard, and merchant navy cadets. Sail training is the most cost-effective and efficient way for young people to learn that the sea is a hard taskmaster. In Canada, a coordinated military sail-training program has never ranked high in political priorities. Budget cuts that closed the Royal Naval College in 1922 launched a cyclical pattern of limited commitment followed by restraint. The onset of the Second World War brought with it additional funding, and HMCS Royal Roads naval college was soon housed on the magnificent estate of Hatley Castle, ideally close to the Esquimalt base.

HMCS Niobe *was the first RCN ship to arrive at her base in Canada. She featured an unusual method of anchor and mooring cable stowage. Circa 1911.*

The recent Korean War reminded the military that conflict was a recurring reality. It and the pervasive fear of communism brought a rapid expansion of Canada's fleet and naval air arm.

A growing navy needs officers. With this end in mind, Captain Bob Welland developed the Pacific Coast Training Plan and was appointed its commanding officer. It was a plan that would bond "the people's boat," HMCS *Oriole,* to the Victoria waterfront forever.

On August 11, 1954, HMCS Venture was commissioned as a shore establishment run by ship's rules. (It was so named because Welland's boss, Admiral Pullen, had once commanded a training ship called *Venture*.) The new

Like the Oriole, *the cruiser* Rainbow *was not new. She displaced 3,600 tons and had a top speed of 12 knots. Like* Oriole, *some of her gear was anchored in another era. And, like the ketch, the* Rainbow *was a capable ship for training new recruits. She was built in 1893, and while she was steam driven, her steering gear was built to sailing-ship standards. Their wheels were large in diameter and thus were as tall as most men; in order to use the leverage, helmsmen were positioned on one or both sides of the wheel. Depending on weather,* Rainbow's *three wheels could employ up to six helmsmen to keep her on course. Three wheels were necessary because she had no steering engine or hydraulic rams to drive the rudder back and forth. Steering engines would not see service until the end of the century. The cruiser's steering arrangement used a chain drive, pulleys, levers, and a stubby rudder head tiller to give mechanical advantage to manual effort.* Rainbow's *memory lives in the name of a Victoria street and a local sea cadet corps.*

school trained junior officers for the regular navy executive and engineering streams, as well as aircrew for the naval aviation section.

After the war, the navy paid off two of its three aircraft carriers, HMCS *Warrior* and *Magnificent.* In Halifax, where HMCS *Bonaventure* maintained a fleet air arm of helicopters and other planes, navy pilots doubled as ship's officers. While Royal Roads streamed officers into the warships, Venture's basic two-year cadet course combined academics with sea time, promoted cadets to midshipmen, then commissioned them as sub-lieutenants.

Classified ads placed in newspapers across Canada solicited recruits with junior matriculation for a special seven-year, short-service appointment. From every Canadian province, Northern Ireland, Hawaii, and California, 123 young men responded to HMCS Venture's motto: A New Undertaking, To Dare and Be Not Afraid. On September 12, 1954, the first cadets settled into the former HMCS *Givenchy* instruction and dormitory barracks, built around a U-shaped parade square near the main Dockyard gate at CFB Esquimalt. Up the hill, hooks from nineteenth-century hammocks still spiked the walls of another classroom in a building known as the "Stone Frigate." The cadets hiked to playing fields near the old Naden Gate on Admirals Road. Cross-country runners travelled to Royal Roads Military College, a former estate on the Colwood waterfront. A friendly rivalry sprang up between the "Royal Roadents" and their counterparts, who joked, "Venturians are officers trying to become gentlemen. Roadents are gentlemen trying to become officers, which is much more difficult."

Venture cadets learned how to handle sail and navigate in *Oriole*. But there were other oppor-tunities to learn how wind and tide interact. Sometimes, they "pulled" in the whalers before breakfast, because that was their only free time. The school's other training vessel, HMCS *Ontario*, cruised farther afield. That first summer, Captain David Groos took one group to Europe, arriving in Copenhagen on July 1. While the *Oriole* sailed for Bellingham, the *Ontario* left Oslo. Other trips went to New Zealand's Bay of Islands, where the cruiser's crane lowered whalers over the ship's side.

Al Horner would one day command HMCS *Oriole*. As a cadet, he sold advertising for the first

First-year Venture cadets lounge on the Oriole *deck during a 1955 training break. The blond man with a crewcut, seated near the front, is Newfoundland's Fred Mifflin, later to become federal fisheries minister.*

The Venturians wore wool serge uniforms, double pleated down the back, and white wool turtleneck sweaters that always smelled of mothballs. Each locker stored two hats in a huge tin. In the summer, white cotton stretched over basic winter black. Off the base, they could wear "civvies," but they were required to wear grey fedoras in case they had to salute an officer. The Venturians devised two stashes to ditch the hated hats. One was outside the base gate by the bus stop. Downtown, the drugstore at "Pusser's Corner," Yates and Douglas Streets, charged a short-term 25-cent storage fee.

Venture yearbook and contributed this editorial observation:

> The RCN has a rain cloud as part of its fleet. This cloud is based on and is considered part of the equipment of HMCS *Ontario*. It has remarkable station keeping qualities, and may be found at any time above and ahead of *Ontario*. Two days after the Venture cruise reached Hawaii, the rain caught up with us. It is believed on the way to Platypus Bay, Australia, where there are no platypuses, or even platykittens. The cloud maintained its proper position, and moored two minutes after *Ontario* dropped her first anchor. The people around Victoria are still wondering where all the sunshine came from so suddenly.

Canadian universities provided another officer-training stream. Young men could earn a commission through the University Naval Training Division (UNTD). West Coast collegians based at HMCS Givenchy trained in the minesweeper HMCS *Sault St. Marie*. Many UNTDs learned how to navigate in HMCS *Oriole*.

An Auspicious Beginning

*I*n November 1954, HMCS *Oriole* assumed her new role as training tender to Esquimalt's HMCS Venture. Her first officers were Venture faculty members. One repair at a time, HMC Dockyard began the *Oriole's* upgrading. Tradesmen installed a new generator and wiring; electric lights replaced candles and oil lamps, and a leaking shaft was made watertight. By mid-January, *Oriole* was ready to go "junketing." Powered by her favourite sailing conditions, a brisk breeze on her beam, she took cadets across the Juan de Fuca Strait for a skiing trip to Washington State's Olympic Mountains. In Port Angeles, an informal U.S. Coast Guard visit foreshadowed many decades of "foreign port" protocol.

At the end of February, the sailboat set out in convoy with two 75-foot auxiliary power craft. Primarily as a pilotage exercise, the three ships transported the Venture football team and its supporters to Vancouver's Stanley Park to play against St. George's private school for boys.

Cadet Joe Cunningham remembers that *Oriole* wasn't the cleanest of ships, but she was watertight. On this first cruise to the mainland, Cunningham and a regular-force leading seaman were her engineers. In mint condition, *Oriole's* engine would have made 7 knots, but wear and tear from pounding into the wind between Mexico and Canada had diminished its efficiency.

As the ketch motored against the strong current in Active Pass between Mayne and Galiano Islands, the exhausted motor sputtered and stalled. Luckily, there was no wind to blow them onto the rocky shoreline, and they weren't being set backward or forward. The obvious option was to anchor, but the officers realized there probably wasn't enough line to put down ground tackle, so they maintained station until the tide turned. The *Oriole* had survived her first West Coast dilemma.

Later, a short trip up Vancouver Island's east coast reconnected *Oriole* with her wartime roots. A cruise with officers and cadets from Nanaimo's Amphion Sea Cadet Corps convinced Captain Bryan Judd to schedule more overnights, because they gave a good opportunity to observe cadets in "other than normal conditions."

In April, *Oriole* buzzed with activity as she prepared for her first West Coast race, the Swiftsure International Yacht Race. Participation in this annual event would become a tradition that endeared the yacht to an adoring public. In the dry dock, tradesmen inspected *Oriole's* propeller shaft and underwater fittings, and sandblasted and repainted her hull. Her crew set to work with sailmaker's palm

As well as Venture's "Number One," Lieutenant-Commander Bryan Judd was HMCS Oriole's *first West Coast commanding officer. He graduated from Britain's training ship HMS* Worcester *on the River Thames at Rotherhithe and saw Korean War action as a deck officer in HMCS* Crusader.

and needle to repair the worn canvas, and checked her rigging. Mechanics fitted cathodes and a hull log. Carpenters scraped and revarnished the wood on her upper deck.

To work up his team, Judd used every excuse to practise and even had them sailing dog watches. For pacing partners, he enlisted yachts like the *Dragoon,* a 67-foot ketch built for the 1926 Bermuda Race and later owned by British movie stars Ronald Coleman and David Niven. On Friday, May 27, 1955, flying ceremonial flags from stem to stern, HMCS *Oriole* announced her racing debut to the northwest yachting community rafted in Victoria Harbour for pre-Swiftsure rituals.

The next day, on the way to the Swiftsure Bank mark, a strong flood tide set *Oriole* backward. Judd left Bob Welland on the wheel and went below to grab some sleep. It didn't last long. A loud crack sent him back on deck to find the bosun and two seamen jury-rigging the forestay. The rising wind had overloaded the large headsail and snapped the bowsprit. "All I remember is going up on deck and shouting at the helmsman to put her downwind," he says. "There were these eager young cadets trying to pull the genoa out of the water. I was worried they would go overboard."

On the run back to Victoria, the spinnaker boom broke in three pieces, splitting the chute. Thirty-nine hours after the start, before daylight on Monday, May 30, HMCS *Oriole* crossed the finish line, placing fourteenth in the nineteen-boat fleet, ahead of five yachts that had retired. "We managed to get about 18 knots out of her downwind," he recalls. "It was scary."

Oriole's first race had confirmed her merit as a training platform. Judd's official post-race report stated that the cadets had gained more valuable sail-handling and seamanship experience over that weekend than would have been possible in many weeks of normal training:

> The fact that *Oriole* finished the race, in spite of all adversities, was due to the very hard work of all concerned, and the expert knowledge of LCdr. P. A. C. B. Baldwin, RCN, who sailed as one of the crew.

Swiftsure also confirmed that *Oriole*'s sails had reached the end of their useful life. Judd's report recommended a new synthetic suit. "Over a period of years, the cost of Dacron sails will be less than sails made of natural fibre because of their greater strength, negligible mildew factor, and the lower

Fifteen years of constant use had exhausted Oriole's *sails and much of her gear. Keeping her in seaworthy shape consumed Bryan Judd's term. He called her first outing "an auspicious beginning" and took along a Victoria marine photographer to record the occasion. Five minutes after James McVie shot his award-winning photo "Slugging Into It," all three headsails split.*

wear and tear on the rigging due to their lighter weight." June maintenance added four metal bands around the upper mainmast to prevent further splitting at the join. A new bowsprit was rerigged, and the whiskers strengthened.

On July 1, 1955, *Oriole* embarked on a training cruise to Bellingham, Washington. In Rosario Strait the wind died, and so did the old diesel engine. As they drifted gently toward the steep shore where it was too deep to anchor, Judd called the U.S. Coast Guard for help and informed

the Maritime Forces Pacific duty officer. "The admiral said to tell me that on no account was I to use the U.S. Coast Guard, but to get *Oriole* back to Esquimalt even if we had to row," Judd recalls. He turned what he calls a "blind ear." The Coast Guard took *Oriole* in tow, and its mechanic cleared the blocked fuel line. "He managed to get it going in time for us to sail into Bellingham under our own steam. No loss of face."

Oriole continued her close encounters with disaster. Midshipmen from HMS *Superb* doused an

1955 Swiftsure Lightship Classic

ACTUAL FINISH P. D. T.

POSITION	YACHT	SKIPPER	CLUB	CLASS	TIME
1	Maruffa	J. Graham	Seattle	AA	13.42.28
2	Westward Ho	J. & W. Helsell	Corinthian	AA	14.32.21
3	Adios	C. Jensen	Seattle	AA	14.49.09
4	Red Jacket	G. Parsons	Seattle	AA	15.37.22
5	Serada	C. Goodhope	Corinthian	A	15.53.51
6	Kate II	D. Skinner	Seattle	A	16.02.55
7	Diamond Head	H. Wyman	Seattle	AA	18.16.31
8	Stormy Weather	G. Teats	Tacoma	A	18.48.43
9	Dorade	F. Eddy	Seattle	AA	19.47.18
10	Polho III	H. Richmond	Seattle	A	21.25.29
11	Totem	H. Kotkins	Corinthian	BB	23.39.00
12	Gometra	E. Palmer	Royal Van.	A	25.05.00
13	Oriole	Lt. Cdr. B. Judd	R.C.N.	AA	28.22.00
14	Armida	K. Hostetter	Corinthian	B	28.53.00
DNF	Dragoon	W. Holms	R. Victoria	AA	DNF
DNF	Escapade	H. Jones	Seattle	BB	DNF
DNF	Yankee Clipper	J. Kelly	Corinthian	BB	DNF
DNF	Mischief	R. Smith	Portland	B	DNF
DNF	Elusive	W. Morrow	Royal Van.	B	DNF

CORRECTED ELAPSED TIME

POSITION	YACHT	CLASS	TIME	CLASS	POSITION	YACHT	TIME
1	Serada	A	23.06.17	AA	1	Maruffa	23.17.34
2	Maruffa	AA	23.17.34		2	Westward Ho	23.20.32
3	Westward Ho	AA	23.20.32		3	Adios	23.56.01
4	Kate II	A	23.21.29		4	Red Jacket	24.52.01
5	Adios	AA	23.56.01		5	Diamond Head	28.17.57
6	Red Jacket	AA	24.52.01		6	Dorade	28.35.29
7	Stormy Weather	A	25.31.33		7	Oriole	39.01.13
8	Diamond Head	AA	28.17.57	A	1	Serada	23.06.17
9	Dorado	AA	28.35.29		2	Kate II	23.21.29
10	Polho III	A	29.05.51		3	Stormy Weather	25.31.33
11	Totem	BB	29.52.00		4	Polho III	29.05.51
12	Gometra	A	32.10.04		5	Gometra	32.10.04
13	Armida	B	34.15.21	BB	1	Totem	29.52.00
14	Oriole	AA	39.01.13	B		Armida	34.15.21

Results of 1955 Swiftsure Classic sailed from Victoria, B.C., to Swiftsure Lightship and return starting May 28, 1955. Sponsored by Pacific International Yachting Association. (Cruising Club of America handicap ratings.)

engine-room fire, apparently caused when a spark ignited gases from the batteries. Damage was slight, but Judd requisitioned a fan to improve air circulation. During an early-September swimming break in the Nahmint River, an able seaman drowned. *Oriole* brought his body to Port Alberni, then sailed home.

Bryan Judd's last sail in *Oriole* happened with one of her most illustrious skippers, Joe Prosser. The cruise down to Seattle with a power craft was uneventful, and they had a good visit with the U.S. Navy. But on the trip back, they ran into a full gale. "The story I heard afterwards was that the duty officer called the admiral because he was worried about the ship's safety," Judd remembers. "He was informed that Judd and Prosser were on board, and if they couldn't get them back then no one could. A nice compliment.

"The only unfortunate thing about my days in *Oriole* was the worry of something happening to one of the twenty-odd cadets in all their keenness because of all the inadequate gear. It put me off any further sailing. Apart from the trip with Prosser, and that was not fun in the end, I never sailed again, and did not teach my children sailing as a result of it."

In December 1955, Lieutenant-Commander Bryan Judd was posted to HMCS *Ontario* as navigator. His successor, Venture Training Officer Lieutenant Robert MacLean, was the first of three "fly boys" to command the navy ketch. The second was his 1944 Royal Roads classmate Geoffrey Hilliard, the third, his student Al Horner.

Cadets from Royal Roads Military College also hoisted *Oriole*'s sails. Her training cruises usually involved auxiliary craft like the Gate vessels *Porte de la Reine* and *Porte Quebec*. On the opening day of the Royal Canadian Naval Sailing Association's (RCNSA) 1956 season, Rear-Admiral Hugh Pullen, Flag Officer, Pacific Coast, launched a club tradition when he reviewed the sailpast from the *Oriole*'s deck.

After *Oriole* failed to finish her second Swiftsure in 1956, Bob MacLean's monthly "proceedings" indicated that nothing had changed.

> The sails are unable to stand the strain of moderate winds, and have stretched so that one cannot point close to the wind. *Oriole* is, in all other respects, capable of giving keen competition to other sailing vessels.

Because the ship was still leased, the navy doled out only enough money for urgent repairs. As the

Bob MacLean taught Venture's aviation component. As an air-squadron pilot, he had landed Sea Fires, Sea Furies, and Trackers on the Bonaventure *flight deck. For two years, he taught basic program to "lower deckers" (non-commissioned officers) at HMCS Cornwallis.*

months flipped by, and the sails and rigging stretched thinner and thinner, it became obvious that one way or another, a decision on *Oriole*'s future would have to be made. Returning the yacht to the Navy League in seaworthy state would cost more than buying her. (A new suit of sails alone was approximately $14,000.) In November 1956, the Naval Board approved the $14,500 to buy *Oriole*, although the transfer papers were not signed until July 12, 1957.

Old Sailors
Never Die

*H*MCS *Oriole*'s most flamboyant captain, Lieutenant-Commander Charles Arthur Prosser, took command in January 1957. No man could have brought more varied experience to the restoration challenges than this feisty mariner who had fed into the Venture executive stream as HMCS *Ontario*'s navigating officer.

"All who know him know he will live on forever in us," eulogized a *New York Times* news item on April 22, 1986. "Old sailors never die." On the waterfront at King's Point, New York, a monument with a sail facing backwards honours the U.S. Merchant Marine Academy's first sail master, Charles Arthur "Joe" Prosser.

The sea was ingrained in Joe Prosser's psyche. He used to joke that he was conceived in a dory. Prosser was born on July 18, 1918, in Gaultois, a Newfoundland outport, and grew up in the "Bankers" owned by his father—great fishing schooners that stacked dories on their decks. Every morning he would row off and handline until the glistening cod loaded his little craft to the gunwales, or the fog closed in, or a storm blew foam off the cresting seas.

At the start of the Second World War, he joined the Newfoundland Commandos and went to Europe. During a raid on a Nazi-held Norwegian base, Prosser was wounded, captured, and held briefly as prisoner of war. He escaped and made his way to England. His commando nickname, "Joe," stuck with him for the rest of his life. Invalided out of the unit, Prosser joined the Royal Navy, a common practice among seamen before the island colony of Newfoundland became Canada's tenth province in 1949. For the rest of the war, he saw action in the Atlantic, Africa, the Mediterranean, and Burma. Starting as a naval rating, he earned a 1943 commission at the Greenwich Royal Naval College and commanded the frigate HMS *Zanzibar*, running North Atlantic convoys.

After the war, he was posted to the Royal Navy submarine school HMS Sea Eagle in Londonderry, Northern Ireland. A 1951 transatlantic passage in their yacht, *Dawn Star*, brought Lieutenant Prosser and his wife to Canada, where he enlisted in the Royal Canadian Navy. From HMCS Cornwallis, then the largest Commonwealth training base, Prosser came west and served in the Korean War.

Before he became captain, Joe Prosser had often joined Bryan Judd on the *Oriole* bridge to show the trainees some old-style seamanship. As her master, the energetic officer quickly earned a reputation for getting things done. He was known as a prodigious "rabitteer," as scroungers were called. If he felt something would be useful, and it wasn't listed in the "rate book" inventory, he would coax the item from allies scattered among the rocky hollows of Her Majesty's Canadian Dockyard. At the end of January 1957, he filed his first official report.

> An inspection of the sails, at present stored in the gymnasium at Venture, was very depressing indeed. It is intended to carry out a further inspection at sea during the month of February. I have the honour to be, Sir, Your obedient servant, LCdr. C.A. Prosser, RCN.

Further sea trials confirmed that *Oriole*'s sails were in a "deplorable state from fair wear and tear." The report concluded, "It was fortunate that the wind did not exceed 20 knots."

A man of independent means by virtue of his wife's wealth, Joe Prosser drove around Victoria in a black Mercedes convertible. When the required sails were slow to materialize, he ordered the new suit himself. In a phone call to the sailmaker, he guaranteed to pay the bill if the navy didn't. This magnanimous gesture earned him lasting fame in West Coast naval lore, which credits him with making good on his promise. Prosser paid to replace *Oriole IV*'s original large wheel with its present version, which is scaled down in diameter.

With his navy blue wool toque pulled down around his crumpled face, the robust mariner set an exemplary standard for the trainees. Faithful to the mariner's maxim of "keeping a weather eye lifted," he looked aloft for fraying lines, whipping that needed renewing, or blocks that needed overhauling. Prompt attention to these small maintenance details prevented major problems. Prosser kept a weather eye on more than the ship's fittings. His March 12, 1957, proceedings advised:

Captain Joe Prosser and crew pose with their catch.

> The crew are untrained from a yachtsman's point of view and this will only be achieved by an extended cruise with that sole purpose in mind. Day sailing is insufficient for an initial breaking in or shakedown for a crew that has never sailed before. Under sail at night presents a totally different picture and will be encouraged before we embark on Spring Training.

His next report compared *Oriole*'s living conditions to the spartan accommodations that the navy recompensed with extra pay, known as "hard layers":

The ship is extremely damp and cold at sea. There is no heating or drying facilities at all. Contrary to popular opinion, I have known men to receive hard layers for more luxuries than exist in *Oriole*. Defect lists have been prepared, and are being processed, but are frustrating indeed when there is so very little that in any way resembles any other form of naval ship or equipment, but yet is subject to the same form of policy. The morale and health of the ship's company remains satisfactory.

May 1957 found *Oriole* "high and dry" while carpenters, mechanics, and electricians scurried to complete her first West Coast refit. The new sails were delayed, but anticipation of their arrival boosted crew morale. Spruced up from stem to stern, the ketch set out on a shakedown cruise to Friday Harbor. Several weeks later, she escorted six RCNSA Sailorette sloops to Port Townsend, at the entrance to Puget Sound, for the annual Pacific International Yacht Association (PIYA) Regatta. Racing skippers scooped the cadets for crew, which gave them excellent small-boat experience. The new sails passed their sea trials admirably.

During Prosser's command, there was one junior officer who had dreamed about the ocean as a sea cadet in Edmonton. Rear Admiral Richard Waller attended Royal Roads and graduated from RMC Kingston. His brief sea time showed him why other countries promote sail training. "I am not a yachtie," he said, "but in *Oriole,* you learn to appreciate the element you are living in. Your eyes are at water level, at times looking up, not down. When you are 45 feet above the water in a naval ship, you still have a certain sense of detachment from the ocean. Every sailor, regardless of rank, should ideally spend some time in *Oriole*."

Prosser organized *Oriole*'s most ambitious schedule. For the next three months, she logged over 2,000 nautical miles under sail and embarked record numbers: 92 Venture cadets; 50 Sea Scouts; 47 UNTDs; 12 Royal Roads cadets; 45 private-school students; 27 civilian dignitaries; and 40 reservists.

Swiftsure 1958 climaxed weeks of preparation, workups, and final rigging tune-ups. Crowds gathered in Victoria Harbour on Thursday, May 29, to watch the annual pre-Swiftsure extravaganza: troubadours on a floating schooner stage; Humphrey Golby's whimsical boat "roll call"; HMCS Naden Band; and a saluting battery fired beside the legislature lawn. Who could predict that this year would be the "Great Calm," the slowest-ever race?

For five hours on Friday morning, the flooding tide pushed *Oriole* backwards towards Trial Island's lighthouse, seven miles behind the starting line. This windless pattern repeated many times over the weekend as she drifted aimlessly or turned lazy circles on the glazed waters. At 7:00 a.m. on Monday, June 2, the navy ketch finished in seventeenth and last place, earning a fifth in AA class on CCA handicap rating.

"We hope you win," encouraged HMCS *Skeena*'s giant placard as *Oriole* left HMC Dockyard for the 1959 Swiftsure start at Brotchie Ledge. Captain Prosser manoeuvred the ketch across the line ahead of the fleet. Their huge genoas drove *Oriole* and her Seattle rivals *Maruffa* and *Diamond Head* to windward as they battled for the lead. Then a loud "bang" aloft announced that *Oriole*'s topsail had burst. Prosser shortened sail, and repairs continued until the wind slackened that night.

Becalmed off Sooke on Sunday morning, the fogbound crew devised a unique way to establish or "fix" their position. They lined up a homemade direction finder with the deck planks and made what they dubbed the "barking dog fix" to locate the

Commanding Officer Joe Prosser was driving HMCS Oriole *when James McVie climbed out on the bowsprit to take this picture during a 1959 Swiftsure "shakedown" crew workup.*

direction of Sheringham Point foghorn. On Whiffen Spit, Victoria Skeet Club shotgun blasts gave them an approximate bearing. The Sooke Harbour House innkeeper's dog verified this information, which the duty watch carefully plotted on the chart. The sounding produced, if not a fix, at least an "area of probability." Race escort HMCS *New Glasgow* confirmed *Oriole*'s position on her radar. She was one mile from shore.

By 1959, the press had discovered the magic "the people's boat" wove in the public imagination.

The Canadian Broadcasting Corporation (CBC) put a cameraman on board to document a day sail for 40 Duncan sea cadets. This segment ran nationally as part of an hour-long special, *Sailing in British Columbia.*

Officer training got a boost when the navy tasked power vessels to support *Oriole*'s teaching role. Built to ferry men between Esquimalt Harbour and the navy's Colwood operations, they were outfitted with many extra navigational instruments, especially for the training program. Operating together on extended training cruises, YFP 312 and HMCS *Oriole* could accommodate twenty cadets, who were divided into equal groups and changed ship every second day. On the yacht, they learned seamanship, sail handling, and pilotage. On the YFP, they received basic instruction in compass and helm, lookout procedure, knots, splices, ship handling, towing, station keeping, and communications.

In the 1960s, Esquimalt offered an alternative officer-training stream so "lower deckers"— the bosuns and the petty officers—could qualify as deck officers in nine months. On one of these courses, a future captain went for his first sail in the ketch. As soon as Joe Prosser found out that Peter Hunter had already put in 22 years' sea time in the Royal Navy and had sailed a whaler from Britain to Gibralter, he handed over the helm to his "student."

Prosser, a gregarious *bon vivant* and raconteur, relished his role as purveyor of the Gooderham "centre of hospitality" tradition. On July 17, 1959, HMCS *Oriole* transported Queen Elizabeth and the Duke of Edinburgh to view the assembled West Coast fleet anchored off the Victoria waterfront. Over the next few years, many senior naval officers signed the guest log. In 1960, for example, Captain Morgon Giles, RN, commanding officer of the Royal Navy Far East Flagship HMS *Belfast,* joined the flag officer, Pacific Coast, in *Oriole* for the Royal Victoria Yacht Club's season-opening sailpast in Cadboro Bay.

Veteran ocean-racing watch captains Rear-Admiral Ted Finch-Noyes and Captain Pratt, his chief of staff, volunteered for Swiftsure 1961. They alternated on the helm after *Oriole* sprinted over the start line ahead of 62 yachts, including the Northwest's most formidable AA Class racers: *Sea Fever, Maruffa, Troubador, Diamond Head*, and *Spirit*. With this expertise driving the *Oriole*, she was well positioned to win, but once again the dying wind left her drifting aimlessly.

The YAGs—the NATO designation for a "training vessel less than 40 metres"—were built in the 1950s as YFMs (Yard Ferry Man) and later called YFPs (Yard Ferry Personnel). They were used as harbour ferryboats and later converted to training vessels for seamanship and navigation. These 75-foot, carvel-planked, 18-foot-wide vessels are 75 gross tons (a measure of volume). The Roman numerals on their grey hulls show the draft (how much of the vessel is under water).

The summer of 1962 bookended Joe Prosser's vigorous tenure. Maritime Forces Pacific designated the Dockyard diving tender YMT 10, *Oriole,* and the yard vessel YFP 312 as the "Auxiliary Training Squadron for Underway Training under the administrative control of the Queen's Harbour Master, and the operational command of *Oriole's* Commanding Officer." A new laminated bowsprit replaced the wooden spar snapped in a sudden squall during the 434-nm MarPac Race on the Washington State coast. The yacht motored to Vancouver, picked up repaired sails from Miller Brothers, and tuned her rigging on the way back. Returning from Seattle's World's Fair, the navy sailors relied on YMT 10's radar in fogbound Puget Sound.

On August 8, *Oriole* and the Auxiliary Training Squadron embarked on a cruise to Alaska. Fog, ice floes, and drenching rain during the 1,832-nm pilotage exercise challenged the navigational skills of 23 UNTD cadets and 20 reserve ordinary seamen. On visits to Ketchikan, Taku, Juneau, Petersburg, Prince Rupert, Bella Bella, and Alert Bay, the men enjoyed U.S. Coast Guard hospitality and northern culinary delights.

It has been said that Prosser resigned his commission in 1964 because he opposed the planned armed forces merger, which he felt would undermine Canada's proud naval tradition. He joined the Caribbean-based Eaton family yacht and in 1965 accepted an invitation to skipper a former America's

Cup defender, *Weatherly*, which had been donated to the United States Merchant Marine Academy. Prosser signed on for nine months. He stayed for 21 years. His presence helped the Academy establish itself as one of America's leading waterfront facilities. He promoted small-craft and sail training as the ideal way to teach seamanship, ship handling, and leadership. Thousands of midshipmen respected this U.S. Maritime Service captain as their role model: his cadets worked hard, because they didn't want to disappoint him.

At his funeral in April 1986, trophies won by his sailing teams covered three tables. Prosser's HMC Dockyard colleague and longtime friend Commander Dick Meadows, RCN (Retired), scattered the old mariner's ashes on Long Island Sound.

In life, Prosser was a much-decorated naval officer, a member of the New York Yacht Club, and life member of the Royal Naval Sailing Association. Named as an honorary alumnus of the United States Merchant Marine Academy in 1984, he was inducted the next year into the Inter-Collegiate Sailing Association's Hall of Fame. The Mid-Atlantic Intercollegiate Sailing Association named its team race championship in his honour.

After his death, the Academy named its boathouse in his memory and posthumously inducted him into the new United States Merchant Marine Academy Athletic Hall of Fame. In 1994, the United States Sailing Association named its highest award for sailing instruction in his memory. And in 2001, the Academy dedicated a Yocum Sailing Center conference room at King's Point as the "Captain Joe Prosser Wardroom." His sword and other mementos are displayed in this room.

One measure of a man's life is the respect and affection of his friends and colleagues. Charles Arthur Prosser will live in our collective maritime memory as the consummate example of loyal,

When Joe Prosser's health failed, his friends bought him a motorized golf cart fitted with a figurehead, compass, steering wheel, and mizzen sail. He liked to dress in full gold-braid uniform and navigate the cart around the golf course.

dedicated service to three countries, and for his devotion to, and compassionate concern for, shipmates and fellow mariners.

In February 1963, *Oriole's* first British Columbia-born skipper assumed command. Lieutenant-Commander William D. Walker graduated from Victoria's Oak Bay High School and saw wartime service in the cargo ship *Windermere Park*, where he earned his second-mate, foreign-going ticket. In 1950, Walker joined HMCS Discovery Reserve Division while he studied at the University of British Columbia. When the navy offered him a commission, he enlisted.

Bill Walker captained with a great singleness of purpose and a profound intuition for the elements and his ship. He would often lie on *Oriole's* deck and watch the shifting cloud patterns to spot weather changes. "He talks to her like a dinghy," said a colleague. Noticing that she was too sluggish for her design, he consulted a naval-architect friend. It seemed that additional ballast had been added on the East Coast to stabilize her as a training platform.

Radical surgery followed. Walker had her keel deepened to lower her centre of gravity, and removed ballast the weight of a city bus. The first sea trials justified this decision. Outside Esquimalt Harbour, *Oriole* scalded away from the harbour craft transporting a photographer, who struggled to document the modifications while they were still within lens range.

Forty-knot gales buffeted *Oriole* during Walker's first major training exercise. In February and March 1964, she visited U.S. naval and coast guard bases in San Francisco, Monterey, Point San Luis Obispo, Santa Catalina Island, San Diego, Newport Beach, Santa Barbara, and Eureka. She carried a public-relations officer, Lieutenant Jack Humble, whose first log entry was recorded at 0900 on Monday, February 3:

> All stores aboard, ship looking trim and neat and straining at her mooring lines. Crew onboard busy stowing kit and finding a place to hide the extra pair of "long-handlers" that "Madam" insisted we bring "just in case." We had a visit from many VIPs, Captain Browne, Captain Leir, Commander Sheppard and Commander Phelps, USN, all of whom wished us well. (I wonder why they all crossed their fingers as they left? Just got no faith I guess.)
>
> The 21 crew included Venture cadets tasked to "Our Ladies Tatting Society," who pushed wax-threaded needles against protective leather "palms" to repair torn sails. Captain, Pole Climber and Abalone Angler LCdr. Bill Walker headed the list, followed by Senior Clockwatcher, laundry and morale officer, wine taster Executive Officer LCdr. Joe Gallant, of HMCS *Margaree* and HMCS *Cape Breton*. Lt. Ian

Sturgess of Liverpool, England was the Navigator, Good Humour Man and Wine Minder. LSBN3 Ed Lascelle was the Coxswain, Tyrant of the Upper Deck and Rum Boatswain; LSBN2 Hank Denksen was the Sailing Master and Bell-Rope Manufacturer; LSEM2 Hank Van Ek was the Engineer, Keeper of the Instant Wind Machine and Bilge Pumper-Outer.

Communications Officer, Navigator's Nagger, and Old Joke Man P1SG3 Ray Negrich earns special mention:

> I feel very remiss in not having mentioned our "voice communicator" earlier. Firstly, having had little or no training in the equipment he was asked to use, he was convinced that nothing short of sheer genius (on his part) achieved good communications, and to hear him trying to explain to the US Coast Guard stations that we were under SAIL (and therefore required a weather forecast for very good reasons) was absolutely out of this world. Such as, "We are under sail … Wrong—I spell—S-A-I-L. We are ketch rigged … Wrong—KETCH RIGGED—not ketch-up." Axis Sally had nothing on our boy. That powerful voice, with super pitch, could only belong to one Negrich.

The entry concludes:

> Life must be looking up; some vicious chess and crib games are now in progress and with blood in their eye the famous cry of "fifteen two and the rest won't do" is ringing around the mess deck. And so with the lights of

Point Cabrillo flashing to port, we finish our last middle watch before entering San Francisco.

On February 17, the *Oriole* arrived at Avalon Bay on Catalina Island, owned almost entirely by chewing-gum magnate Mr. Wrigley. Three ship's divers inspected *Oriole*'s hull. They found no faults, but surfaced with enough abalone to feed the ship's company. The next day in San Diego, the navy ketch lay alongside the USS *Koka*. Bill Walker's April report noted:

Needless to say, our hosts could not have been more gracious. The two crews became as one. It was not an uncommon sight during the forenoon scrubdown to see a U.S. sailor, barefooted, scrubbing down with our own hands. Washers, dryers, showers and the evening movie were all much appreciated by *Oriole* personnel.

That summer, onshore emergencies called time-outs from *Oriole*'s schedule. Off the west coast of Vancouver Island, the Canadian Fishing Company at Nootka lost its electric power as the fishing fleet was coming in. The navy sailors soon had the generator working again. During a Gulf Islands cruise, the sailboat crew helped Salt Spring Islanders put out a brush fire at Stonecutter's Bay.

Thanks to Bill Walker's dedication, his successor inherited a meticulously maintained, seaworthy ship.

Oriole's West Coast Skippers

Lieutenant-Commander Bryan Judd	November 1, 1954–December 5, 1955
Lieutenant-Commander R. C. MacLean	December 5, 1955–January 6, 1957
Lieutenant-Commander C. A. "Joe" Prosser	January 6, 1957–February 18, 1963
Lieutenant-Commander W. D. "Bill" Walker	February 18, 1963–May 3, 1965
Lieutenant-Commander James Butterfield	May 3, 1965–August 18, 1967
Lieutenant-Commander Geoffrey Hilliard	August 18, 1967–July 26, 1969
Lieutenant-Commander Peter Cox	July 26, 1969–February 26, 1971
Not Manned	February 26, 1971–September 25, 1972
Lieutenant-Commander Al Horner [R]	September 25, 1972–July 16, 1973
Lieutenant-Commander R. D. C. Sweeny	July 16, 1973–August 10, 1973
Lieutenant-Commander W. D. Walker [R]	August 10, 1973–June 7, 1981
Lieutenant-Commander Peter Hunter	June 7, 1981–May 4, 1983
Lieutenant-Commander James R. Gracie	May 4, 1983–October 15, 1984
Lieutenant-Commander Peter Watt	October 15, 1984–August 29, 1988
Lieutenant-Commander Ken Brown	August 29, 1988–August 2, 1991
Lieutenant-Commander Michael Cooper	August 2, 1991–May 18, 1904
Lieutenant-Commander Michael J. Brooks	May 18, 1994–June 21, 1998
Lieutenant-Commander Larry Trim	June 22, 1998–August 15, 1999
Lieutenant-Commander Scott Crawshaw	August 16, 1999–present

LIFTS AND HEADERS

Sea Fever

> I must go down to the seas again, to the lonely sea and the sky,
> And all I ask is a tall ship and a star to steer her by, …
> —"Sea-Fever," by John Masefield

*T*he *Oriole* was still plying Great Lakes waters when sea fever propelled James Butterfield to the shores of Vancouver's Burrard Inlet, 2,000 miles to the west. The young James watched the continuous stream of deep-sea traffic and dreamed about sailing to the Orient in an *Empress* liner. In the 1930s, Canadians pursuing a merchant marine career had to travel to Britain for officer training. When he was thirteen, Butterfield overcame his family's concerns, boarded a train for Quebec, and sailed for Britain. He celebrated his fourteenth birthday as a cadet in HMS *Conway*, John Masefield's alma mater, which was anchored in the Mersey River. Then he apprenticed aboard the SS *Empress of Russia*, built in 1912 for

Canadian Pacific to compete on passenger routes to the Orient. The *Empress of Russia* was one of four *Empress* ships taken over in 1940 by the British Admiralty to serve primarily as troop transports.

Early in the Second World War, one circuitous run took the *Empress* from Egypt to Britain via the Caribbean and the east coast of the U.S. In Suez, a young British naval officer named Philip Mountbatten embarked—Philip of Greece and Denmark, later the Duke of Edinburgh. In Newport News, Virginia, one of the largest east-coast coaling ports, some 90 men—an entire watch of stokers—deserted. The *Empress* burned 270 tons of coal every 24 hours, all stoked by hand. When the call went out for

The Empress of Russia *outward bound from Vancouver Harbour. Inset: Lieutenant-Commander James Butterfield, circa 1960.*

volunteers to trim the coal and tend the boiler fires, Mountbatten and Butterfield and their watch mates wrapped their heads in towels to cope with the sweat and shovelled their way to Halifax, where they were relieved by Royal Canadian Navy stokers.

Butterfield switched to cargo vessels and was second mate in *Jasper Park* when torpedoes sent four men down with the ship south of Madagascar. Back in Canada on survivor leave, where every radio station was playing the song "Roll Out the Barrel," he went down to the Vancouver recruiting office and joined the Royal Canadian Naval Reserve (RCNR) for professional mariners. For the second time, Butterfield boarded a train for the East Coast. In Halifax, the navy immediately posted him as navigator in HMCS *North Bay,* which was escorting convoys from "Newfie John" to Londonderry.

In addition to yachts, naval officer-training programs had access to Second World War ships,

including Canadian-built shallow-draft Algerines designed to carry fuel and depth charges. HMCS *Sault Ste. Marie* and Butterfield's original command, HMCS *Border Cities,* were deployed to the West Coast. The Nova Scotia-based HMCS *Portage* and *Wallaceburg* ranged eastward to Toronto, sometimes pairing for exercises. In 1952, and coincident with the short-lived Nova Scotia career of HMCS *Oriole,* two men who would become closely associated with "the people's boat" were assigned to the same Algerine. Butterfield was first lieutenant in the *Portage*, and the training officer was Joe Prosser. Butterfield fondly recalls the friendship that formed between them aboard the *Portage*. "She was a small ship, so we saw a lot of each other."

Portage cruised as far as Quebec's Gaspé Peninsula, and training exercises followed a regular pattern: an overnight anchorage, a major sea port, and a small port for the weekend. Learning signals, practising skills, cleaning the ship, and writing up their journals for the staff to mark occupied the cadets. Prosser varied their lessons to evoke rivalry among the UNTDs from across Canada. Conducted largely by a series of flag hoists that kept the students scrambling, these instructional contests were generally good fun for those who entered into the spirit of the games.

True to his home-town spirit, Joe Prosser believed in fun. To celebrate Butterfield's 35th birthday, the pair went on a "run ashore" to Grand Falls, Newfoundland. Prosser knew everyone. "The first thing you know, we were besieged," Butterfield

recalls. "Joe told all his buddies it was my birthday. We set to and had a party, in the course of which his friends dashed about to their houses and produced photo albums of young Joe in the battleship HMS *Malaya*."

His time on the East Coast would provide Butterfield with valuable experience when he entered the West Coast officer-training stream.

In May 1965, after fifteen years on both coasts, James Butterfield went from first lieutenant of the navy's largest vessel, HMCS *Provider*, to commanding officer of the smallest, HMCS *Oriole*. As she and the training squadron cruised northward along Vancouver

In 1945, James Butterfield joined the Royal Canadian Navy and started training for his commission. In 1950 he went on course to England. As opportunity allowed, he explored the waters around Southampton in HMS Dryad's sail-training sloop. Obtained through war reparations, Planet *still flew her wartime swastika below the British ensign. Meat was still rationed, and Dryad's agricultural facilities on a former estate continued their wartime poultry production. "We would pack our weekend's goose ration, and off we'd go," he recalls. Butterfield's first peacetime command was the wooden-hulled Bay Class minesweeper HMCS* Fundy.

Island, crews rotated at designated towns. While the yacht sailed up the volatile outside waters, the YFPs powered up the sheltered eastern shore. Once, a thick seasonal fog bank closed in on *Oriole* before sunset, which made for an interesting night, as the crew had to stay alert to prevent an accident. The next day, she motored down the saltwater fjord to Port Alberni, where her cadets boarded a naval bus and traded places with their YFP counterparts at Nanaimo.

In late June, *Oriole* again sheltered overnight from the heavy fog. With 1,500 fishing boats reported between Cape Beale and Tofino, it was not prudent to stand off the coast under sail in the fog with little wind and a working crew of nine first-year cadets. On the next rotation, the YFP went to Campbell River, and the trainees rotated at Gold River. "Some didn't get much sailing time, and consequently had no real idea about sails doing anything but flapping in the breeze," comments Butterfield. "But now and then, we had a nice beat to show them that yachts don't need engines to move about in the water."

Seattle sailors had organized a NorPac racing series along the Juan de Fuca Strait. The race committee set a new course every day. *Oriole* was a keen participant. During one event off Ucluelet's fogbound Amphitrite Point, she had a close encounter with an old rival, Henry Kotkins' ketch *Diamond Head*. "We both had to let fly and go hard over to avoid a collision," Butterfield recalls. One leg of the race went from Bamfield to Tofino, where the yachts tucked into an isolated anchorage behind Meares Island. "I don't know how in blazes he did it," says Butterfield, "but our cook, on something like half an hour's notice, whipped up a birthday cake, which was brought up on deck with all due ceremony, pipes trilling, and was much enjoyed by everyone during the evening."

Joe Prosser would go on to leave an indelible mark on Canada's West Coast and at the U.S. Merchant Marine Academy in New York.

Butterfield left the navy in 1967 to work for the British Columbia Ferry Corporation. By the time he retired twenty years later, he was senior skipper for the *Queen of the North* on her northern run from Port Hardy to Prince Rupert.

Her next captain proved that given a strong, steady wind, *Oriole* was unbeatable. As a new graduate into the post-war military, Lieutenant-Commander Geoffrey Hilliard inherited a world in which the shooting was winding down. Hilliard grew up in Picture Butte, Alberta, graduated from Royal Roads in 1944, and boarded a Halifax hospital ship bound for the Japanese war theatre. But by the time they got there, the war was pretty well over, so Hilliard joined HMS *Duke of York* and saw first-hand the ruins of Nagasaki. In addition to his naval commission, Hilliard was a trained pilot. He expanded his knowledge with a course at Portsmouth's HMS *Excellent*, qualifying as the Fleet Air Arm's only gunner.

By 1962, Hilliard's progression up the ladder had taken him back to the west, as executive officer in HMCS *Saskatchewan*. When a colleague turned down the *Oriole* command, Hilliard volunteered, then marvelled, "Are they going to pay me to do this?"

For a California cruise, Hilliard invited along a man who would become captain of the *Oriole* some twenty years later. "I went along because I was interested in sailing, and Geoff wanted a diver on board," says Ken Brown. They bashed into typical rough winter weather, especially when crossing the "Potato Patch," a shallow spot just north of the Golden Gate where the seas build up and generate a lot of surf. "We went up one of those waves and down it. There were two of us fighting the wheel to keep her true," Brown recalls. Hilliard, too, was a shallow-water diver. In San Francisco, both men donned scuba tanks and dove down to check out the rudder. "We had cranked her hard coming across this Potato Patch, and [the captain] wanted to make sure we hadn't bent anything," says Brown.

In the 1960s, new fibreglass technology generated significant waves in the boating marketplace. Mass-produced yachts replaced traditionally built wooden hulls, flooding the sport with thousands of new sailors and creating a marina-building boom. During this rapid transition, Geoffrey Hilliard inaugurated what would become another *Oriole* tradition: participation in a new offshore event.

When the first Vic-Maui gun fired in 1968, the steel-hulled ketch, under Hilliard's command, started

During Geoffrey Hilliard's final weeks as captain, HMCS Oriole *collected her first racing trophy. On July 27, 1969, five yachts set out from Port Angeles on a 565-nm mini-ocean race to the Cobb Sea Mount south of Cape Flattery.* Oriole *led around the mark; steady, powerful winds pushed her across the Neah Bay finish line sixteen hours ahead of Ralph Higgins' Victoria sloop* Gabrielle II. Oriole *also won overall honours on corrected time by ten hours. However, she had blown out most of her sails, so Hilliard had to send for thread to repair the damage before she could join the NorPac racers in Barkley Sound.*

among a composite fleet of thirteen "woodies" and glass boats. One unusual mid-ocean Mayday brought a presidential apology from Lyndon B. Johnson. *The Mouse That Roared* author Leonard Wibberley radioed race escort CNAV *Laymore* that "an unknown U.S. Navy warship" was shelling his yacht, *Cu Na Mara*, and later quilled on parchment a complaint to the White House. During this race, Doug Fryer listened to *Oriole's* daily radio broadcasts in his 34-foot cutter *African Star*. "In those days, the regular navy still had a tot of rum issued during the day," he recalls. "She had a happy hour when the guys would get on the

Officer cadets are seen here at work and at play during Captain Hilliard's command. They had fun saluting other yachts with their "grapefruit gun" (top left and bottom right) and also found creative uses for the spars (bottom left).

air and entertain the fleet with songs and poems." Fryer sighted the steel ketch in the latitude of Los Angeles. *"Oriole* came out of the clouds on a day when we both logged long distances."

Glamorous ocean races notwithstanding, most training exercises hugged Canadian shorelines. One shimmering summer afternoon, when half of Victoria was out for a drive, a friend phoned Hilliard's wife, Heather. "You've got to go down to Clover Point," she burbled. *"Oriole*'s on the rocks. She's got the most beautiful bottom!" Sure enough, there was the good ship listing to port, stranded by the falling tide. A Dockyard tender rushed Ken Brown and a diving team to check for damage. A smaller craft also responded, winding the towline around her propeller in her haste. Without power or steerage, YMT 10 was in far worse shape than the object of her rescue and drifted out to sea on the ebbing tide before she could untangle the rope and return to the base. *Oriole* floated free on the flooding tide and motored back to her jetty.

On February 1, 1968, the three separate services—Royal Canadian Air Force, Navy, and Army—merged. When Lieutenant-Commander Hilliard ended his career with Dockyard's event-planning staff, he was the last serving officer still wearing "blues." Although he was in charge of drilling, he couldn't go on parade with his men because he didn't own the new "greens." And because he wasn't going to be there much longer, he said he would be damned if he was going to buy a new uniform.

Geoffrey Hilliard died in a diving accident at Malta in 1977, when he and his wife, Heather, were enjoying a retirement cruise in their Dutch barge, *Sophia*.

Bottom of the Food Chain

"When funds are allocated, *Oriole* is always at the bottom of the food chain. In times when the purse strings are tight, it's hard to quantify [the value of] sail training in an era when technology rules. In the cyclic swings, *Oriole* pops to the top of the list," says Admiral Richard Waller, RCN (Retired).

Following the merger of the three services, federal restraint slashed military budgets, robbing Lieutenant-Commander Peter Cox of the chance to share his considerable old-school experience with young sailors. Born in the British Columbia Kootenays, Cox spent the war as a boy seaman in the North Atlantic. He earned his bosun's commission at Portsmouth, where he trained in the "boom defence" performed by MarPac's Gate vessels.

After Cox transferred from the NOTC Venture faculty to command *Oriole* in 1969, the purse strings tightened rapidly. Staffing was a continuous challenge, and Cox had to tap the base-manning pool for crew. "Nobody could supply us with funds," he says. "I'd have to scrounge to get replacements for the engineer, cook, cox'n, and sailing master." Austerity also restricted *Oriole's* cruising range, but somehow the purse strings loosened enough to fund her entry in a slow 1970 Vic-Maui Race that lasted three weeks.

By the time Cox retired in February 1971, the money flow had dried up. "They didn't replace me," he says. "Perhaps they needed all their officers and men for other ships, so it was easier to lay her up than maintain and operate her." With HMCS *Oriole* mothballed at her jetty, rumours swirled, and Victoria businessmen dreamed about forming a syndicate to buy the navy's longest-serving vessel for a charter boat.

In 1949, Admiral Ted Finch-Noyes had asked Ottawa Naval Headquarters for money to help the West Coast Naval Yacht Club acquire new boats. His leadership spearheaded a coast-to-coast recreational sailing network for armed forces personnel. When a 1952 order-in-council created the Royal Canadian Naval Sailing Association (RCNSA), Esquimalt Squadron, Peter Cox was its first vice-commodore. After the three forces unified in 1968, RCNSA became the Canadian Forces Sailing Association (CFSA).

Maintaining and sailing the RCNSA's Sailorette fleet built teamwork and provided continuity for the fledgling club. As a group project, members bought lumber from a bankrupt mill and built Snipe sailboats. At the same time, they acquired three Sailorettes from Hunter Vogel's dismantled Maple Bay Boatyard and finished them.

In the spring of 1972, an unexpected request launched a reversal in the *Oriole*'s fortunes. CFSA civilian dinghy sailors dreamed of entering her in Swiftsure and asked CFSA Commodore Peter Hunter to approach Admiral Leir, the chief of staff. After much discussion with Leir, permission was granted. Terms specified that after the race she would be unrigged and returned to "bare-bones" condition.

Hunter was also commanding officer of the Fleet Maintenance Group and its flagship, HMCS *Cape Breton*, a 10,000-ton Victory Class cargo ship that the navy had converted into a repair shop complete with a foundry and giant lathes. This wartime freighter also doubled as a hotel for crews while their ships were in refit, her galley dishing up meals on an assembly line.

Hunter cast his critical professional eye over the forlorn *Oriole* languishing at her jetty and declared, "We just can't do this." Restraint had stripped her gear. Not a bit of running rigging was left. Her radios were gone. Below the upper deck, her salon was awash in a green mildew that coated the antique upright piano, carpet, upholstery, and bulkheads. None of the heads worked. Fuel was contaminated, and the batteries were flat.

But the indomitable CFSA sailors decided that, with help, they *could* do something. The rule was that as long as they didn't use Dockyard money, they could do anything they wanted. Scuttlebutt circulated through the kelp grapevine, and *Victoria Times* waterfront reporter Pat Dufour got wind of the project. "I told her to keep quiet," says Hunter, "and she did." As specified, no federal money was spent. Dockyard electricians, riggers, and tradesmen came in on nights and weekends, working on their own time.

In 1972, there were two divisions in the 138-nm course to Swiftsure Bank. In the International Offshore Racing (IOR) fleet, the Vancouver

Lieutenant-Commander Peter Cox made a lasting contribution to Canada's sailing community. He helped West Coast naval officers lay the groundwork for the Royal Canadian Naval Sailing Association (RCNSA), Esquimalt Squadron, which gave HMCS Oriole the mandatory club affiliation to race in Pacific International Yachting Association (PIYA) and other major events. Over the decades, this military sailing club has also provided a venue for Oriole crew members to enjoy small-boat racing and recreational sailing.

12-Metre *Endless Summer* (the former Australian America's Cup challenger *Dame Pattie*) scored three trophies: first around the mark; first across the line (shaving two hours off *Maruffa*'s 1957 record); and overall winner on corrected time.

Larry Mofford and Frank Piddington in the Sailorette Green Teal *in 1954. In 1946, George Owen designed the 27-foot Sailorette Class with minimal cruising accommodation. Between 1949 and 1952, the RCNSA acquired seven of these traditionally planked sloops, named them for sea birds, and painted their hulls in matching colours. Dockyard Fleet School apprentices built* Golden Gull. *Over the next four decades, the one-design fleet flew the RCNSA and CFSA burgee in many area regattas.* Green Teal *travelled to Japan as deck cargo in HMCS* Provider *and cruised the Inland Sea. As easy-maintenance fibreglass hulls accelerated the demise of wooden yachts,* White Swan *and* Blue Goose *were declared surplus and destroyed. A 50-year era ended in 2000 when the navy returned* Red Start, Black Hawk, *and* Silver Heron *to Crown Assets.*

Peter Hunter was supposed to skipper *Oriole* in Swiftsure's Pacific Handicap Racing Fleet (PHRF), but another priority intervened. There was no lack of volunteers, however: former captains Peter Cox and Jim Butterfield, and top CFSA Fireball dinghy tacticians Jack Stacey, Dennis Carlow, Hardy Lane, and Doug Bond. They conscripted an army cook for the weekend, who persevered through bouts of seasickness to produce clam chowder and pies. Sail Master Stacey remembers that there was no place to cool the pies, so they stowed them in a cutlery drawer, where "everything intermingled." The CFSA team brought *Oriole* home in less than 27 hours, placing eleventh in the 29-boat PHRF division.

The next week Hunter had planned to get the gang together to strip the ship back to the promised bare-bones condition, but *Oriole* got a reprieve. Twenty-two young sub-lieutenants returning from courses at England's Manadon Military Engineering College had no place to stay. The B.C. Lions summer football camp occupied Royal Roads Military College; NOTC Venture and the Naden Wardroom had no empty beds.

"We said, 'Ah! *Oriole*!'" recalls Hunter. These temporary billets cemented the upward progression in *Oriole*'s fortunes. From then on, her fortunes improved rapidly, and she eased back into active service.

The *Oriole* Sails

How do you build a sail that equals the combined area of five small houses? With great ingenuity. Vancouver sailors Sid and Phil Miller figured it out. In the 1930s, at Vancouver's Kitsilano Yacht Club on English Bay, the brothers built and raced Geary 18s and Star boats. After the Second World War, they campaigned their 6-Metre *Ca Va* out of the Royal Vancouver Yacht Club. In the late '40s, they pioneered British Columbia's first indigenous sail loft. When *Oriole* came west, the local loft was an obvious choice for keeping her sail inventory in good repair.

Second-generation sailor and sailmaker Dave Miller carries on the family traditions. His father and uncle were Olympic trials runners-up. Dave represented Canada in Tokyo, 1964 (Star Class); Acapulco, 1968 (4th Dragon Class with Steve Tupper); and Kiel, 1972 (Bronze Medal Soling Class with John Ekells and Paul Cote).

Building *Oriole*'s spinnaker, which is the size of a football field, presented a huge challenge. The sailmakers solved the problem by laying it out on the ice at the Vancouver Forum. "We would roll the cloth out and hold it in place by pressing our palms on the ice," says Miller. "It melted, so when you took your hand away, it would freeze it in place." They laid out her main and genoa sails on the arena ice, and also pressed other large areas into service, including the second-floor dance hall of Hamilton Street's old Legion building and Stanley Park's HMCS Discovery drill hall.

Miller Sails became North Sails Canada in 1974; it is now wholly owned by North Sails. Since the mid-1980s, North Sails has built most of *Oriole*'s sail inventory. "It takes a while to get to know her characteristics and idiosyncrasies," says Miller, "which means going out in the boat." He gained insight by joining *Oriole* on several Swiftsures. "She is a very heavy boat and needs to have a lot of inner sail area compared to her weight. Her genoa has a very long foot. Her mizzen sail plan is relatively large and works very efficiently upwind and downwind. Her mizzenmast has a reverse load and bends back, so the sail needs to be flat."

Oriole's sail loads require very strong fibres that can control the stretch. Initially, her working sails were 7-ounce Dacron and 1 1/2- and 2-ounce nylon. The newer fabrics allow genoa weight to get down to 5 ounces, which is very light for that large a sail. Her latest working main and mizzen sails are made of a Spectra Mylar laminate. They are constructed with a radial rather than crosscut configuration, which controls the stretch and distributes the loads better. More sail area and more roach were added to the main and mizzen leech.

Sail Inventory
Yankee (high-cut jib)
Jumbo (storm sail)
Genoa
Mizzen staysail
Three spinnakers (3/4-ounce, 1.5-ounce, 2.2-ounce)
Two gennakers (1.5-ounce, 2.2-ounce)

Top: Skipper Larry Trim manoeuvres HMCS Oriole *during a light-airs 1999 Swiftsure start with an Adventure Training crew of Winnipeg engineers. Bottom left: Buffer Dave Greene supervises crew in spinnaker set during 2000 Adventure Training cruise. Bottom right: "Jiggering down" the backstay during Swiftsure 1999 workup.*

Top left: NOTC Venture officer cadet Underhill on HMCS Oriole *foredeck in Marlborough Sounds. Top right: Buffer Al Cottrell gets into the hula spirit during 1990 Vic-Maui race. Bottom: Assistant sail master Andy Sage supervises gennaker repacking on the dock at Friday Harbor, Washington State, during September 2000 Adventure Training cruise.*

Top: Oriole *encountered a lot of floating ice in Alaska's Tracy Arm. Bottom: HMCS* Oriole *flies the world's largest Canadian flag on the way to OSQAR 84.*

Top: HMCS Oriole was host vessel for CISM Chiefs of Mission during the first week of June 2001. A competing yacht sails behind a Canadian Forces YAG carrying the CISM Race Committee officials. Bottom left: A team official samples the midday smorgasbord set out on the Oriole's coachhouse roof. Bottom right: Guests watch as Martin 242 yachts head for the leeward mark during a day of CISM 2001 racing.

Top: HMC Dockyard fireboat Firebrand *salutes old and new technology as a Sea King helicopter escorts* Oriole *in the 1980s. Bottom: Fisgard Light guards the entrance as CISM sailors approach the leeward mark inside Esquimalt Harbour.*

CFSA is the host club for the Victoria Chapter of the Disabled Sailing Association. HMCS Oriole often benefits the disabled. Top: "Raising Sails for the Kids" takes youngsters in wheelchairs to watch the annual Lions Society of B.C. Easter Seals Regatta, which raises money for children's summer camps and other projects. Bottom: Skipper Larry Trim celebrated with newly married 2000 Mobility Cup champion John McRoberts and his bride Vivian after their 1999 wedding ceremony aboard HMCS Oriole. The couple's dog, Moondance, rests on the deck. During the international 2001 CISM and Mobility Cup regattas hosted by CFSA, Vivian was a volunteer on Race Chairman Paul Ulibarri's committee.

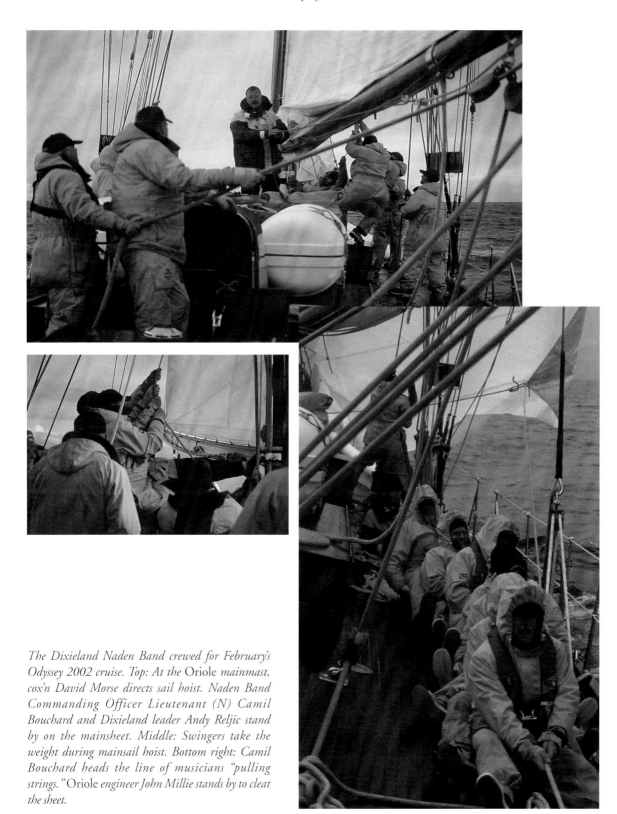

The Dixieland Naden Band crewed for February's Odyssey 2002 cruise. Top: At the Oriole *mainmast, cox'n David Morse directs sail hoist. Naden Band Commanding Officer Lieutenant (N) Camil Bouchard and Dixieland leader Andy Reljic stand by on the mainsheet. Middle: Swingers take the weight during mainsail hoist. Bottom right: Camil Bouchard heads the line of musicians "pulling strings."* Oriole *engineer John Millie stands by to cleat the sheet.*

Top: HMCS Oriole *and* Bluenose II *pace each other in the Strait of Georgia in 1986.* Oriole IV *and the first* Bluenose *were launched on the Atlantic coast in 1921. Right: Marine and military artist Pierre De Wispelaere's painting of* Oriole, *commissioned by an Australian naval officer who had sailed in* Oriole.

Odin Tames
the Grommets

Her next commanding officer had watched HMCS *Oriole* arrive from Halifax. "They mustered the duty watch and marched us down to the float," recalls 1954 Venture cadet Al Horner. "Whereupon this dirty great sailboat came out of the murk, and sort of appeared. Everybody was trying to tie it up properly, and of course didn't have a clue." Eighteen years later, Lieutenant-Commander Al Horner, Staff Officer Reserves, Fourth Training Squadron, accepted one of *Oriole*'s most interesting commands. Returning from a sailing holiday, he was told that Admiral Richard Leir planned to recommission *Oriole* and wanted him as her captain. The fact that Horner was "only a reserve" didn't seem to bother anyone.

Horner brought valuable experience to the challenges. After a Halifax posting as a Fleet Air Arm pilot with Geoff Hilliard, he returned to the West Coast. By 1970, Horner was senior commanding officer for the Gate vessels *Porte de la Reine, Porte Quebec,* and *Porte Dauphine* and training coordinator for western naval reserve divisions. "Thrilled to bits" with his new command, he started from scratch. Scrounging regular-force seamen from other ships, he hammered them into a crew and started to put the ship back together.

The officer-training program also had to start from scratch. Before his 1970-1973 appointment to Maritime Pacific Command, Rear-Admiral Richard Leir was Ottawa's senior officer in charge of officer recruitment and training. His department embraced military colleges and men on both coasts, so all training plans landed on his desk. Observing the effectiveness of MarPac's Venture and Fourth Training Squadron programs—*Oriole,* three Gate vessels, and four YAGs—and the East Coast fleet—*Pickle, Grilse,* and *Tuna*—Leir hoped to revive the West Coast training squadron. "I looked very favourably on that," says Horner. "I thought it would be neat. Unfortunately, it didn't come about."

For as long as *Oriole* had been out of the loop, junior officers had trained at CFB Chilliwack on the Fraser River east of Vancouver. In 1973, Horner informed the press, "They come out knowing all kinds of air force things and army drill. They are good at square bashing and learning to be managers, but they don't know the ship's head from the galley." He tailored his new program so that men who had never seen salt water could appreciate coastal tides and weather. "We have a lot of managers in the forces," he explained, "but we also have to develop leaders. There is no better way to become a leader than to work in this ship."

In the late 1940s, the Royal Navy and Royal Canadian Navy sail-training programs acquired German yachts that were termed "prizes of war." Three went to Halifax. During the war, the 59-foot Luftwaffe training yawl *Heligoland* was bombed to the bottom of Kiel Harbour. She was resurrected and sent first to Britain, then to Canada. Shipped across the Atlantic as deck cargo and renamed *Pickle* (right), she was berthed at HMCS Shearwater. Navy crews raced her frequently. She flew the Royal Canadian Naval Sailing Association burgee in a 760-mile open-ocean race from Newport, Rhode Island, to Bermuda, placing 21st in a field of 89. Lieutenant-Commander P.A.G. (Casey) Baldwin was among her crew in the Manchester-to-Halifax race. The navy used two ex-German sister ships, the 38-square-metre *Grilse* (top right) and *Tuna* (top left), in Halifax in its sail-training program. Navy crews raced them in regattas that often drew record entries in an era that predated mass boat-construction techniques.

Seeking exercises that would develop leadership, Horner got permission to plan for the Rio de Janeiro-to-Plymouth leg of the Whitbread Around-the-World Race. A likely rotation would have taken one crew down, exchanged in Rio, then again in Plymouth for the return via Halifax and Panama. Ottawa had already set the wheels in motion to get foreign port clearance.

It was not to be. A hull inspection revealed several paper-thin steel plates. Electrolysis causes corrosion in salt water. Because zinc corrodes faster than steel, placing sacrificial zinc pads on the outside helps to keep the hull sound. But while *Oriole* was laid up, renewing these pads had been neglected, and until the corroded plates were repaired, she was not allowed to sail offshore.

Horner set up a six-week sail-training rotation. After the basic officer course, cadets went out in *Oriole*, then finished their practical sea training in the minesweepers or destroyers. Clad in drab dark-green work dress, white turtleneck sweaters, and running shoes, the trainees spent their first week day sailing. They learned how the rigging worked, how to handle lines, raise and lower sail, and tie knots. They studied rules of the road, basic coastal navigation and pilotage. One of their first seamanship tasks was to build a lanyard belt out of small line fastened with spliced Inglefield clips (small hooks) to hold their spike and line-cutting knife.

For the next five weeks, the *Oriole* cruised. On the way to Desolation Sound, Horner dropped the hook in anchorages used by Captain George Vancouver. In mid-coast fjords they practised "ancient sailor stuff," relying on sound instead of radar. To centre the ship in mid-channel, they made a loud noise and listened for the echo. Some gear still needed upgrading. Their depth sounder came off a chain-store shelf. Because the anchor windlass was neither hydraulic nor serviceable, they installed

an intricate series of blocks along the main boom to control the anchor rode as they paid out the line.

Horner tried to instill an appreciation for living off the land. At Refuge Cove, some cadets used the dinghy for fishing and clam-digging forays. Others climbed the hill behind the cove, where wild strawberries, salmonberries, and mint flourished. Their army field cook fed them well, often preparing fresh salmon and squid. Using every scrap, he kept a soup pot simmering. Horner recalls, "There was an awful lot more of us at the end than the start."

For their graduation leg, the cadets sailed night and day to reach Seattle by the weekend. Horner put them in charge of navigating and choosing the right sails for the wind conditions. If they decided to wear more sail than was wise, they had to justify it and ask permission from the watch captain. *Oriole* tied up at Lake Union's U.S. Naval Reserve building, where Dick Wagner established the Center for Wooden Boats a few years later and a berth for the retired Swiftsure Relief Lightship and old timber carrier *Wawona*.

The dicey part was threading the Crittenden Canal into the lake. Going through the locks was an excellent navigation and seamanship exercise, and included the challenge of numerous bridges. Using appropriate sound signals, *Oriole* had never had a problem until late one night when an operator failed to realize the height of her mainmast and didn't fully open the bridge. The crew had to put the mast in the opening and steer to the middle, altering course as the stick entered the gap. The sight of a mast running light at the same height as the control tower galvanized the operator to action. It is questionable whether the bridge ever opened as fast before or since.

On one return from Puget Sound, a stiff breeze festooned *Oriole* with freezing rain and snow. Ice coated the sails. Icicles formed under the main and

Lookout Al Horner, a Venture cadet, straddles the bowsprit of Oriole *in 1955. He returned as captain in 1972 (inset).*

mizzen booms, and along the guardrails and pulpit. Ice glazed the deck. "It was not fun, but interesting from the point of view of having done it," recalls Horner. He tried to minimize spray by reducing sail to the Yankee and mizzen, which balanced her nicely. Coming about just before they dropped the mainsail, a pocket opened, drilling a batten into the deck by Horner's foot. He conceded and motored the rest of the way home, although in those weather conditions *Oriole* handled more comfortably under sail.

The press noticed HMCS *Oriole*'s absence from the 1971 Swiftsure and headlined her return to regular competition in 1973 "THE OLD LADY IS BACK." Previous reports of "sloppy sail handling" coming from the comfort of an aircraft or powerboat led Horner to organize a special cruise for the press. *Victoria Times* reporter Peter Salmon chronicled the trials of the "half-lubber" crew. "They have blisters on their hands today to prove that sailing the *Oriole* is not a pleasure cruise," he wrote. "Six newsmen more used to handling microphones or typewriters than inch-and-a-half-diameter rope braced themselves on the deck." Along with five acting sub-lieutenants who had just completed basic Chilliwack "army-oriented boot training," the scribes learned what it was like to haul on a rope until it would move no farther.

On CKDA "Fresh Sound, Mostly Music" letterhead, John Mackin reported:

Oh, life on the bounding waves sounds all very great and very romantic. I'm just not sure I am equal to it. I ache in every bone and joint I possess. It took me about fifteen minutes to summon enough mobility to press the elevator button in my apartment building. They had me hauling on sheets and lines and halyards. And in one day I am only half dead … When you see the *Oriole* in the Swiftsure and you watch her coming about or changing sail, you will know a crew of eager young men are racing around like bee-stung orangutans working their hearts out … *Oriole* separates the boys from the men in a hurry. They've been working eighteen hours a day and regard it as a privilege and honour to be aboard. Crazy … from the captain, Al Horner, right through the crew, there is a closeness and a camaraderie that you won't find anywhere else.

On race day, *Oriole* started well up in the pack. Flying everything but the lead line, she rounded the mark at five in the morning and cut so close to *Porte de la Reine*'s anchor cable that the helmsman had to take corrective action to miss it. She was halfway down the Strait when the wind died. "We hummed and hawed our way until Monday morning and then sailed home. Disappointing, but on the other hand, it was fun," remembers Horner. "If you're not having fun, then why are you doing it?"

Horner credits two expert old-time seamen with the program's success. "I had absolutely no problem when cox'n Don Bota was on watch. I could always count on him to keep me informed about other vessels or hazards if it was my time to sleep," he says. "And buffer Keith Hanna worked very hard himself, and also worked the kids hard. There was no sitting around on a long tack. He'd have them whipping lines. Bota gave all the new junior officers nicknames as part of their initiation. The kids loved him. There was Kamikaze. Smiff with two effs. Cookie Monster. Newf. Log Frog. In the middle of the night on deck you would hear, 'Smiff one eff, where are you?'" The kids called Bota "Smiling Buddha," but not until they had graduated from *Oriole*.

After one shore leave, the cox'n and buffer brought Odin back to the ship, complete with food and toys and a litter box, which they kept in their head. "The first I knew of it was four thirty in the morning leaving Seattle," says Horner. "This shadow came bouncing through the curtain into the captain's cabin and onto my shoe, with all claws extended. I almost had a heart attack." With perfectly straight faces the culprits confessed, "It's a cat, sir." Thus the *Oriole* acquired a mascot named for the Norse god of wind and war.

Very much a sea cat, Odin lived all over the boat. Sometimes he would leap off the jetty, end up in the drink, and have to be fished out. A couple of the "sub-looies" created a proper "pusser" hammock for him—a little rectangle with seven lines to the end of the canvas, which they slung between the mast and the forward bulkhead. On sunny days, Odin would walk out on the main boom and curl up in the belly of the sail. Someone would stand by to scoop him out as the boom came across. When the watch changed, he would sit above the hatch and bat the berets of the junior officers as they emerged from the companionway.

When new trainees came on board, the crew explained that the cat was along to keep the grommet* population down. The cox'n lifted his feet and shouted, "Grommets," whereupon the regular crew followed suit. Newcomers quickly caught on to the joke. As the cox'n usually trailed a line over the stern, the crew seldom ate fish that wasn't fresh. Yet the captain kept finding cans of pusser beef, tuna, and salmon. When asked why, the cook's explanation was simple: "For the cat, sir."

After his *Oriole* captaincy, Al Horner commanded Victoria Naval Reserve Division HMCS *Malahat*. Starting with Walter Owen, he was aide-de-camp to five lieutenant-governors of British Columbia.

(*A grommet is formed by whipping a line's ends into a circle.)

Greybeards

A greybeard is an old wave that goes around and around the globe, never touching land, building up a terrific weight before it crashes on itself. This is what makes Cape Horn so rough. Like this ancient wave, Bill Walker went around and around the Atlantic and Pacific Oceans at the helm of Canadian Navy training yachts.

In 1965, Lieutenant-Commander William Walker transferred to Halifax as the deputy chief of staff and served as commodore of the Royal Nova Scotia Yacht Squadron. In 1968, he took *Pickle* and a crew of new RMC Kingston graduates on a race from Bermuda to Travemunde, Germany. Between Cork and Land's End, the watch captain, Petty Officer Glen Shippam, lay on the deck and listened to the historic broadcast of an Apollo lunar mission. Later, as senior hull surveyor at HMC Dockyard, Shippam supervised *Oriole* repairs.

Walker retired from the navy for the first time in June 1971. For years the family had planned their boat. Nothing but a schooner would do. Walker bought a Doug Roxborough hull in Nova Scotia, finished her interior, and rigged her. The Walker children painted, scrubbed, and varnished, cooking meals on weekends so that their mother, Marion, could help with the boat. Finally, the Walkers embarked in *Chebucto* for British Columbia.

For three weeks in August 1973, Lieutenant-Commander Roger Sweeny captained *Oriole,* until Walker, now a reservist, assumed command for the second time. Once again, his leadership brought stability and progress. Money was still scarce, so surpluses from other Dockyard budgets were redirected to ensure the yacht's survival. To keep costs down, cadets volunteered their spare hours for work parties, which often ended in the captain's dining room, savouring one of Marion's roast beef dinners.

Oriole followed the Gooderham tradition of frequent visits to American ports. In 1976, she featured in Seattle's U.S. Bicentennial celebrations and led the May 1 sailpast on Lake Washington to officially open the Seattle Yacht Club's new facilities. Because he preferred to wait for the wind to fill in, Bill Walker used very little fuel. As a result, customs officials occasionally collected overtime pay. During frequent Gulf Island training cruises, the cadets sometimes slept ashore in tents at the Walker cottage on Pender Island, which his father had homesteaded after he retired from the Royal Navy.

In 1977 and 1978, *Oriole* underwent major overhauls. A three-month refit replaced corroded main deck crossbeams and the hull plate around the engine exhaust. A lot of rust had developed when water dripped between the insulation and the steel shell, where thickness varies between 3/16 and 1/4 inches from the upper deck down into the turn of the bilge and keel, where the "sheer strake" is thickest. (*Oriole* was built with a centreboard, so her keel forms an integral part of the frames and hull.) The new sections had to be welded, because men no longer worked as riveters. New communication and safety gear was installed: a Decca 060 radar, Loran "C," a Sealand 30 VHF, two echo sounders, and a single sideband high-frequency radio.

In another major overhaul, teak brought from the Far East in HMCS *Provider* replaced worn deck planks. The upper deck boards were removed, allowing daylight to flood into the interior through angled steel deck beams spaced a foot apart (the originals were iron). Around the fittings, where scrubbing and sanding had worn down the wood, the old teak was as much as a quarter-inch thicker than the deck. New planks were attached with special screws.

HMCS *Oriole* starred in 1978 Captain Cook bicentennial celebrations. She sailed to Hawaii to another bicentennial event that pitted her against the boat of an old rival, Vancouver skipper Lol Killam, one of the founders of the Vic-Maui Race. Perhaps his Nova Scotia South Shore ancestors incubated the "blue-water bug" that bit him. To replace his mahogany-hulled sloop *Velaris*, Killam designed a tough fibreglass boat that could withstand abuse from careless crew and pounding waves. Using a pulp-mill construction, he stiffened the hull of his new 73-foot sloop, *Greybeard*, with tremendously strong, square fibreglass stringers.

A reception on board Honolulu Harbor's square-rigged museum ship *Falls of Clyde* brought together crews from *Oriole, Greybeard,* and the communications boat, Victoria writer John Manning's Tahiti ketch *Gungha.* The sailors learned

that the North Pacific High was centred 400 nautical miles farther north than usual for that time of year.

On June 24, 1978, the race to British Columbia that matched *Greybeard* against *Oriole* started in light winds off Diamond Head. Constant tension stretched the navy's synthetic halyards, jiggers, and sheets thinner and thinner, requiring hourly tightening. Otherwise, the masthead moved forward, and she fell off the wind and sailed poorly. Favourable weather held for two weeks. Flying an awesome sail combination for the 25-knot wind— mizzen, mizzen staysail, main, jumbo, genoa, and big spinnaker—the *Oriole* logged 282 nautical miles for her best 24-hour run. Cox'n Keith Hanna describes one trick: "You would be on the helm with everything flying, and you could tell if you were off course by the position of the bird on the spinnaker. You would hear, 'Tail, tail' or 'Beak, beak, beak.'"

The pressure forced the hull down until all 91 feet skimmed the water. Seas curled over her transom as the ship hummed with an adrenalin-pumping vibration that made sleep impossible. Walker says, "You could be in your bunk, attempting to rest, and twenty seconds later be on deck, as alert and wide awake as it is possible to be."

Steering required total concentration. Walker reduced rotations on the wheel to twenty minutes. While *Greybeard* sailed a Great Circle course for the Juan de Fuca Strait, *Oriole* threaded between two pressure systems, as close to the wind as she could sail and still carry the spinnaker.

Two weeks later, *Oriole* arrived at the Strait entrance. When the wind lightened that evening, the crew worked every puff for six hours. Walker's log concludes, "We gybed the spinnaker and set and reset the mizzen staysail, Lord knows how many times, to no avail. Finally, with the assistance of the flood tide, we crossed the line at 1500 hours. Boat for boat, we had finished a day ahead of *Greybeard*."

HMCS Oriole *circa mid-'70s. "When you have her sails set properly and she is balanced nicely, she dances. She's got this little lilt," says former captain Al Horner. "You can be quite confident in heavy weather when she's going like a steam engine. You know that she's looking after you."*

Cook's ships Resolution *and* Discovery *are pictured in this reproduction of John Webber's 1788 drawings from his visit to* Nootka Sound. Captain Bill Walker recreated this tableau with HMCS Oriole *in 1978 for a CBC documentary.*

That August, *Oriole* sailed to Nootka Sound, where a CBC crew filmed a Captain Cook bicentennial documentary called *As Far As Man Could Go*. Along the way, she visited Port San Juan, Bamfield, Ahousat, Clayoquot Sound, Hot Springs Cove, Friendly Cove, and Resolution Cove, where she Mediterranean-moored at Bligh Island. Walker's 1978 historical report notes, "We positioned the ship in accordance with Webber's painting in exactly the same position that Cook moored *Resolution*. The director and I sat on the same rock that Webber sketched from: there was the same snag identifiable in the painting with distinctive crooks and bends sill standing. It gives one an uncanny feeling of not having been established very long." The ship also hosted the film crew in Hilo, where they filmed the Hawaiian section.

In 1979, *Oriole* entered the biennial TransPacific Yacht Race from Los Angeles to Honolulu. Eighty-four boats entered that year, the largest number since the first race in 1906. Before she left the dock, the navy ketch had already claimed six honours: the only Canadian and the only military entry; the oldest boat; the largest in displacement and length; and carrying the most crew. The week before they embarked, all hands helped prepare for the voyage. They learned about letters of credit, cash advances, canteen stores, duty-free stores, naval stores, victualling stores, mechanical and electrical maintenance, how to repair sails and rigging, and how to stow stores correctly. This training paid off in mid-ocean: working for two days in shifts around the clock, two men pricked a trail of tiny 1/8-inch stitches to repair a spinnaker tear.

At San Francisco's Treasure Island, U.S. Navy hospitality taught the trainees about foreign-port protocol and military "host ship" liaison. Shore leave reinforced the message that daily shipyard routines are demanding when you have to be on deck at 0800, regardless of the previous night's revelries. In Los Angeles, the cadets began to appreciate the public-relations aspect of *Oriole*'s mission. Dressed

Promotion was automatic when Bill Walker joined the navy as a sub-lieutenant. During his last two years in Oriole, *he was promoted to commander. It was the custom to "pull" the outgoing captain away from his ship during the annual fleet regatta. Dressed in eighteenth-century cutaway jackets, red-and-white-striped shirts, and white breeches, cadets rowed Commander William Walker and his cox'n, Chief Petty Officer Keith Hanna, ashore in the navy ceremonial cutter on June 7, 1981.*

in tropical white "longs," they mingled with 1,000 yachtsmen at a gala Biltmore Hotel reception, where they impressed the veteran sailors with their nautical knowledge.

Offshore, alert watch captains picked up on serious mistakes as their charges scanned sea and sky for wind, watched the barometer for pattern breaks, drew weather maps from coded messages, and interpreted steep millibar gradients. Five windless days forced the entire fleet to reassess their provisions. To keep busy and add variety as morale ebbed, the cadets created an anonymous radio station. Every day they broadcast ten-minute shows with fake news, weather, and sports. When they confessed to their caper at the awards banquet, the *Oriole* crew drew louder applause than the winners.

For Acting Sub-Lieutenant A. Williams, the race had realized a childhood dream. "I know for sure if I ever have an opportunity of bringing a destroyer alongside," he wrote, "as I prepare my plotting, if someone tells me there is 15 knots of wind abeam, I'll know exactly what that is and the possible effect on the ship." His shipmate, Acting Sub-Lieutenant T. Paterson, concluded, "We saw how the Americans work, and this taught us appreciation for our friends and allies down south. I might just add that everywhere we went the U.S. Navy treated us like royalty. When we left Long Beach Harbor to start the race, the Canadian destroyers of the training squadron signalled, 'You are No. 1, ORIOLE.' I have never been so proud of my country as I was then. The trip was worthwhile for that one event alone."

THE GLORY YEARS

Barometer Rising

*L*ieutenant-Commander Peter Hunter restored HMCS *Oriole* after she had lain idle between 1971 and 1972. The last Second World War veteran to captain the ship, his career followed a traditional pattern. Joining the British Navy as a Boy Seaman Second Class, he served in warships on the Burmese, African, and Russian runs and escorted the first convoy of planes to Murmansk in 1941. Post-war British naval policies hastened his departure for Canada, and by 1954 he had advanced to chief petty officer in the Royal Canadian Navy in the C Class destroyer HMCS *Crusader*. Coming west, he earned his commission from Esquimalt's RCN Preparatory School and later became its director of officer candidates. When Hunter retired in 1973, the Maritime Pacific Command asked him to set up

the Small Boat Unit's YAGS and three Gate vessels. He ran the division for eight years.

When Hunter took over command of *Oriole* from Bill Walker in June 1981, her budget was minimal. The captain shared executive responsibilities with Freeman Abbott, the coxswain, her only other permanent crew. If one or the other was absent, the ship couldn't sail. Abbott was a sea cadet from Burin, Newfoundland, who had enlisted in 1965 and come west in the navy's first tanker, HMCS *Provider*. Hunter recalls, "Freeman was one of the finest seamen I ever knew, with a tremendous sense of humour." The designated engineer came early for a short training session; the rest of the crew arrived on the morning of the first day of the training session. Abbott supervised the upper deck. The cadets cooked and navigated. "Every morning we gave them a different job," says Hunter, "and that's what they had to do for the day."

Technical problems persisted. The valiant engine struggled through three speeds: full ahead, full astern, and stop. A wire beside the wheel went down through the deck and into the engine room, where it rang a bell. "Twice the wire broke when I was going alongside," says Hunter. "Another time the bell jammed. You can imagine where she is tied up now, with her nose up against the road, and suddenly the wire breaks when you ring for astern." Hunter painted three pieces of wood: white for stop, red for stern, green for ahead. "We would throw it down the hatch and hit the cadet engineer with it."

Hunter was determined to bring *Oriole* back to her former high standard. Dockyard could deliver superb workmanship, because many of the old European shipwrights, carpenters, and joiners were still around. Peter Hunter's son, Nigel, was a shipwright. "I put in to have all this nice stuff done," says Peter. "I'm very fussy about boats, and if things weren't done exactly as I thought [they should be], I would tell the guys. So they would say, 'If that fussy old bugger is gonna get on to anybody, let him get on to his son.' As a result, Nigel did the tiddly work, like the companionway and mahogany rails."

Operating funds were still scarce, and there was no money to enter the 1982 Vic-Maui Race. Training exercises were confined to poking into little bays close to home. Hunter always took along three or four experienced hands on weekend and other short trips. "I never took a drink the two years I was on that ship," says Hunter. "If it blows up in the middle of the night, you can't afford to be groggy."

Mariners measure time differently than landsmen. The ships they have sailed collate life's important spans, not months and years. No man can tally more blocks of *Oriole* time than Petty

Lieutenant-Commander Peter Hunter helped to restore Oriole *to active-duty standards.*

Officer Roger "Doc" Beaudry, who fed into the stream during Hunter's command. During 40 years as a senior navy medic, Doc served in a dozen ships on both coasts. Although he was never part of the core crew, the short, wiry Montrealer was posted temporarily to *Oriole* on and off for some twenty years, whenever he could be spared from another vessel. "I trained most of these guys on the helm," he says.

In Halifax, a master mariner taught Beaudry how to sail in ship's whalers. His teacher was Casey Baldwin, whose seamanship skills and eccentricities made him an Atlantic legend. Baldwin never wore a belt; instead, he wound tarred marline rope around his waist to form a distinctive cummerbund—one that also blackened the bottom half of his shirt. It was his working uniform on the open bridge of the old Tribal Class destroyers.

"He was never married when I knew him," says Beaudry. "His dog Six-O and his parrot were his whole life. In those days, the navy had a senior watch-keeping officer, and that's what he was. He would send Six-O home for the night while the ship was in harbour. I remember quite often being on night duty. A taxi would come up and the driver would say, 'I'm here to pick up Lieutenant-Commander Baldwin's dog.' The parrot stayed on board."

Beaudry says that if everything is set up so she is well balanced, *Oriole* is very easy to sail. At sea or in the Juan de Fuca Strait, however, she needs speed to tack through any swell. "If she is well sailed, she handles like a big dinghy. If not, she can be a pig and won't do anything. She has to keep moving."

Beaudry rates a Swiftsure with Peter Hunter as his most exhilarating ride. Glen Shippam was watch captain, and Beaudry was watch mate and helmsman. On the Sunday afternoon of the race, trailed only by CFSA clubmate *Passing Cloud,* Brian Walker's Roue-designed schooner, *Oriole* rounded the Swiftsure mark second to last and headed to the American shore. A stiff westerly filled in. Flying the staysail, mizzen staysail, spinnaker, and small genoa, she broad-reached down the Strait at 15 knots and reached Race Rocks in record time.

Peter Hunter worked with many so-called incorrigible youth and emphasizes that they were "great" on board the ship. One young girl wouldn't speak to anybody. Hunter sat beside her on the hatch and asked her if she had ever been on a ship or held the wheel of a car. She said her uncle used to let her hold the wheel. "When I put her on the wheel, she became a chatterbox," Hunter recalls, "and told me how she wanted to get into computers. The teachers and students were incredulous. Then they clapped because it was the first time they had heard her voice."

By the time *Oriole's* oldest captain "swallowed the anchor," Peter Hunter had put in 44 years in the navy. "I was the only person in the service who stayed around until he was 60," he says. "They forgot about me." In May 1983, Victoria *Times Colonist* reporter Pat Dufour and a photographer covered his retirement party. From the ketch anchored in the middle of Esquimalt Harbour, Venture cadets rowed Hunter to shore in the navy's ceremonial cutter. Contrary to post-unification protocol, the white ensign under which he had so proudly served fluttered from the stern.

Operation
OSQAR 84

*F*or several years, Maritime Pacific Command had been working out logistics to send HMCS *Oriole* to the East Coast for a major tall ships rendezvous. To prime the publicity pump for OSQAR—*Oriole* Sails to Quebec and Returns—Commanding Officer Lieutenant-Commander James Gracie organized a media cruise. In the wardroom, the assembled scribes learned that the ship would be away for seven months and would participate in three tall ships races during the 450th anniversary of Jacques Cartier's arrival in New France. The affable Gracie wore his public-relations role as comfortably as a wet-weather jacket. "Most of these trainees have never been on the ocean before. No sense filling the ship up with experts," he quipped. "They would only argue with the captain."

On March 19, 1984, grey skies canopied the bridge as HMCS *Oriole* embarked to retrace the route that had brought her west 30 years before. Executive Officer Lieutenant Jean-Guy Nadeau, one of three core crew for the entire trip, was also the navigator. The next day, 30-knot squalls churned 13-foot swells, driving sheets of rain across the deck. It was a rough initiation for the air force, army, and navy volunteers from central Canada and the two sea cadets from Calgary and Thunder Bay.

Three days out, off the Oregon coast with a 30-knot southeasterly on her beam, disaster struck.

With an explosive crack, the upper half of the mainmast toppled over the ship's side. Still supported aloft by the main brace, the broken end pounded *Oriole*'s side. For almost three hours, all hands scrambled to retrieve the spar and lash it securely on deck so the ship could return to Victoria for repairs. Rear-Admiral Gordon Edwards later credited Freeman Abbott's leadership with recovering the entire mast and rigging.

For years, the Esquimalt Dockyard had stockpiled fir, anticipating an eventual spar replacement. First, the shipwrights built a sturdy timber bed the length of the shop. Working in twelve-hour shifts, they cut diagonals in various lengths, so the scarf joins would not weaken the entire structure. For flexibility, the mast was hollow, except for a 1/2 metre at the butt and 2 1/2 metres at the top. It was sealed with cold-cure epoxy. Thirty men glued the spar together. Three coats of exterior varnish and an inside coat of shellac protected the wood.

On April 12, *Oriole* set out again. Could she still rendezvous with the tall ship fleet in Bermuda for the race to Halifax? Powering made up for lost time, as did bypassing or cutting short scheduled port visits. The first crew change on April 12 boarded four regular-force men from Halifax, Saint John,

Commanding Officer Lieutenant-Commander James Gracie (right) and Executive Officer/Navigator Lieutenant Jean-Guy Nadeau against a backdrop of Victoria's Empress Hotel as HMCS Oriole *begins her March 1984 "media cruise."*

and Esquimalt; twelve NOTC Venture trainees; and two sea cadets from Stewart, B.C., and Vancouver.

Gear failures continued. The engine's main circulating pump failed. A short-circuit knocked out the navigating instruments. But the new mast survived the next gale. On April 18, winds gusting to 55 knots tossed the ketch like a cork, tore the mainsail, and hammered the crew huddled on deck. Twenty-foot rollers picked her up and set her down abruptly. Secured to the deck, the spinnaker boom broke loose, broke the guardrails, beat on the hull, and threatened to destroy the pin rail and starboard shroud.

Sail Master Freeman Abbott was a short man who moved cat-like and sure-footed around the heeling deck. Dismissing the gale as "50-knot breezes," his jokes broke the tension and boosted morale. With her mainsail dropped, *Oriole* steadied under mizzen and jumbo. Ten hours after it began, the storm was over. "When I went to my bunk in the morning I felt a little more like a real sailor, and had learned a lot of respect for the sea," cadet K. Lewis wrote later in the Esquimalt base's newspaper *Lookout*. "Whoever coined the phrase that sailing was a mixture of boredom and sheer terror wasn't all that wrong. I have a whole naval career ahead of me. If I can learn as much each week as I have this one, I'll do alright."

South of California, the winds took a siesta, while the sun baked the crew in 40-degree heat. Wherever she tied up, *Oriole* attracted crowds, who pointed and asked questions in rapid-fire Spanish. At Puerto Madero, Mexican naval hospitality

Cox'n Freeman Abbott directed the quick action that secured a broken spar and prevented further damage before HMCS Oriole *returned to Victoria for repairs.*

refreshed the crew. At Punta Arenas, Costa Rica, the ship lay alongside for two days. Bearing fresh fruit, the lads returned. "I can still see the expression of horror on the face of our cook, Leading Seaman Harkness, when he opened his fridge and found a fifteen-pound watermelon sitting on a case of eggs," wrote Lewis.

At Panama's U.S. Naval Base Fort Rodman, Lewis reported, "As in the past they treated us like brothers, helping in any way they could, and providing very nice military lodgings ashore." For three days, Abbott and buffer Steve Graham spent most of the daylight hours suspended in a bucket high up the mast, fixing fittings that had plagued them since Long Beach. In spite of the heat, they remained aloft, with only periodic refreshment and country-and-western music to sustain them.

On May 31, HMCS *Oriole* tied up in St. George's, Bermuda. Two days later, 32 tall ships left Hamilton for Halifax. The larger ships headed out to sea in search of wind. The smaller ones set a course for Nova Scotia. *Oriole* worked her way up to the front of the fleet, only to have the wind die. "For myself and others," wrote Lewis, "there was a sense of loss. I'm one of many Canadians who stands taller and [whose] chest swells when ski racer Steve Podborski wins, or we score against the Soviet hockey team. I was hoping to be part of another Canadian victory but it was not to be. On the bright side, there are more races and *Oriole* and her people will never stop trying."

Three days later, northwest of Bermuda, hurricane-force gusts battered the fleet. The navy sailors battened down, reduced sail, and rode out

As a teenager, Freeman Abbott honed his skills on the Newfoundland coast.

the storm. The British barque *Marques* sank in less than a minute, and nineteen sailors drowned. The *Maclean's* cover story "The Tall Ships and the Untamed Sea" quotes a captain who had skippered *Bluenose II* between Halifax and Bermuda many times. "'A squall is not uncommon in those waters. If that wind hit too hard and broadside before they could get her sailing in the direction of the wind,' said Ellsworth T. Coggins of Canning, Nova Scotia, 'she would turn over.'"

Sixteen regular navy and NOTC cadets arrived for crew change on June 12 and donned "*Oriole* whites" for the next day's Parade of Sail. Thousands lined Dartmouth and Halifax shores and cheered as 41 tall ships from 20 countries filed past the reviewing vessel, HMCS *Assiniboine*. As a good-will gesture, some exchanged cadets. *Oriole* gained a

Polish Sea Scout from the *Zawicza Czarny*, who communicated in sign language, and a Royal Navy midshipman from the ketch *Halcyor*. Two *Oriole* trainees joined the Soviet *Kruzenstern* and the Polish square-rigger *Dar Mlodziezy*.

Rain drenched *Oriole* on June 25 as she arrived in Quebec City, towing the 40-foot German yawl *Peter von Danzig*, which had no auxiliary power. At that time, *Oriole*'s engine room could not be called high-tech. Its overworked Cummins diesel engine complemented an old British Lister diesel generator that supplied electricity. Leading Seaman Steve Halliwell replaced engineer Master Seaman R. W. MacDonald for the return trip. Halliwell was a versatile mechanic who could fix almost every problem with his shipwright, welding, mechanical, carpentry, and sheet metal skills. Sleeping in the

In June 1984, the navy ketch welcomed more than 40,000 visitors across her deck. In the wardroom, Prime Minister Pierre Trudeau and his son Justin signed the guest book. With flowered lapel, the prime minister chats with Lieutenant-Commander James Gracie and Freeman Abbott (left).

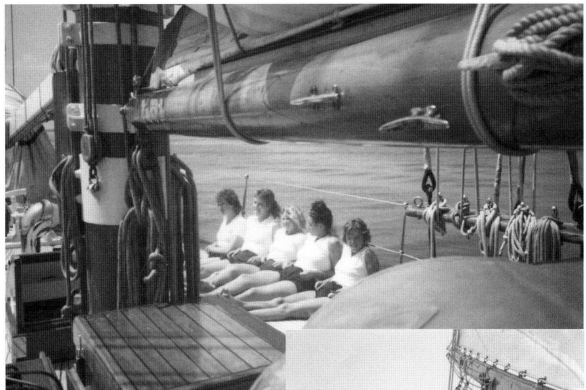

Oriole's *first female trainees came from army, navy, and air force units in Winnipeg, Saskatoon, Gagetown, Cornwallis, Quebec, and Alaska. Three were sea cadets.*

engine room, which then had no bulkhead, he could reach from his bunk and touch the motor. "I went to bed with earplugs on," he says. "I'd wake up and my face would be black."

On July 14, 1984, a crew change for the Halifax-to-Massachusetts leg of the return trip to Victoria opened a new era in HMCS *Oriole*'s saga: her first female trainees boarded.

Heading back south along the Atlantic coast, *Oriole* put in to Baltimore Harbor during a four-day visit to Maryland. For the occasion, Captain Gracie ordered all sails dropped except the trademark "bird" spinnaker. Her grand entrance impressed the waiting Baltimore Orioles baseball delegation. At the next port, the crew exchanged courtesies with their counterparts at the Annapolis Naval Academy.

As they continued toward the Caribbean, Abbott was surprised that the women were equal to the physical work. "They did a fine job," he says. "No doubt about it." Each got one sink of fresh water every day for personal hygiene. The psychological triggers were not so easy to predict. On the way to Florida, as *Oriole* tried to outrun the hurricanes, one stormy night around three in the morning a gust laid the ship right over in the water. She righted, then slammed down on the other side, throwing Abbott out of his bunk. He grabbed a flashlight to make his rounds and checked the bilges to see how much water they had taken on. In the focs'le, he found the girls on the floor, all bundled up with blankets and pillows and mattresses.

They asked, "What happened, Cox?"

"Nothing," he soothed. "Go back to bed."

"Well, what could I say? They were scared to death, because water came in too. Things settled down after that."

After an uneventful Caribbean passage, the *Oriole* cleared the Panama Canal and changed course

for the lumpy ride up the west coast to Canada. Late summer is not the best time for a yacht to be sailing off Central America, especially when she is heading north. In the morning and evening, the watch scanned the horizon with binoculars, alert for the line squalls that produce gusts, heavy rain, and often thunder and lightning. Steve Halliwell sighted half a dozen localized waterspouts ahead in a storm line. "You don't know which way to go to get between them or around them," he says. "Inside, the winds can be high."

Along the Mexican coast, *Oriole* sailed close to the shore, so she could tuck in to a protected harbour in a hurry. Shortly after she left Acapulco in late September, Hurricane Palo formed. Packing 124-knot winds, the storm parallelled the yacht for a week on a track 200 nautical miles farther out to sea. Off Puerto Vallarta, Halliwell patched an exhaust leak, which held until they could repair it at Mazatlán. This extended stopover gave Palo a window to get ahead of them. The hurricane petered out in Magdalena Bay, but would have coincided with *Oriole*'s entrance had she arrived on schedule.

In late August, Lieutenant-Commander Peter Watt and his new cox'n, Petty Officer Ernie Peaker, had flown to Panama for their "change of command" orientation leg to San Diego. Watch captain Doc Beaudry went with them. On October 10, *Oriole* tied up at the Canadian navy's California "home away from home" for a welcome six-day "R & R" and resupply. The next week, Peter Watt took command, and James Gracie flew to an Ottawa posting.

North of Santa Barbara, navy wool toques and yellow survival suits replaced long-sleeved turquoise jackets on the deck watch. *Oriole* powered up the coast against strong northwesterly headwinds and mountainous seas. Nadeau noted, "With the short,

The Berthday Party

On January 13, 1985, HMCS *Oriole*, bearing area mayors and dignitaries, and two YAGs carrying 60 media and guests, triumphantly motored into Victoria Harbour. From her starboard deck, Victoria's Dixieland Express minstrels serenaded, and *Canada I* crew member Eric Jespersen raised the Canadian Challenge battle flag, a beaver in boxing gloves. "Victorians went wild in their welcome," wrote Victoria *Times Colonist* reporters Pat Dufour and Derek Sidenius. "The spectacle rivalled Swiftsure at its grandest." Their arrival celebrated Victoria's designation as a training venue for the next America's Cup Challenge. For this event, the three navy boats had escorted Canada's 1983 America's Cup challenger, *Canada I*, from Sidney, with designer Bruce Kirby and Challenge adviser Dave Miller sharing the helm. In a few months, veteran American helmsman Buddy Melges was scheduled to arrive with his "Heart of America syndicate." Some 20,000 souls cheered as plumes from two fireboats misted *Oriole, Canada I,* and her entourage of 300 small craft. As the flotilla passed Fisherman's Wharf, sound ricocheted around the basin: a cannonade from Laurel Point and the Naden Band on the dock.

jerky motion and constant heel, life below decks was very uncomfortable. Credit must be given to the 'chef,' PO2 Ferguson, for producing meals in even these conditions."

On October 28, 1984, HMCS *Oriole* sailed into Esquimalt Harbour after her longest deployment: 18,285 nautical miles; 235 days; 45 ports visited; and 88 days in harbour.

Fair Winds

*H*MCS *Oriole's* next two commanding officers maintained the blue-water momentum generated during the ship's East Coast ambassadorial voyage.

A former deck officer in HMCS *Provider,* Lieutenant-Commander Peter Watt captained HMCS *Oriole* in the 1986 and 1988 Victoria-Maui Races. Cox'n Ernie Peaker remembers how the first five days in 1986 caught the navy ketch in "one hell of a blow." Rough weather battered the ketch and kept the full watch on deck. Peaker and Doc Beaudry looked after the upper deck, while the rest of the crew members found their sea legs as the ketch plunged through the 25- to 30-foot waves that washed two guardrails overboard. Everyone had a turn on the helm at night. "It was excellent training for the Venture cadets," comments Peaker. "It brought them out of their shells and gave them confidence. It made them into excellent sailors."

In the final 24-hour approach to the Maui finish line, every yacht predicts its arrival time. Beaudry's watchmate, navigator/training officer Scott Crawshaw, was teaching celestial navigation to the officer cadets. He won the Andreas Schueller Memorial Trophy for the navigator with the nearest ETA at 25-mile call-in.

The famous Nova Scotia schooner *Bluenose II,* under the command of Captain Don Barr, visited the West Coast in April 1986. Returning from a visit with *Bluenose II* in Nanaimo, *Oriole* encountered high winds in Victoria's Baynes Channel. Leading Seaman Pat O'Hara recalls the winds clocking between 60 and 70 knots. "Peter Watt told me to keep our course between the two lights, Fiddle Reef and Lewis Reef," he says. "It took two of us to steer, me and Doc."

Peaker observes that in the open ocean, *Oriole* is a very small platform, especially in heavy weather. "She's the safest ship in the navy," he says. "You know exactly what she is going to do. She rides the waves very well if she is well sailed. She is an excellent old girl. She would find pockets in rough weather to sail very smooth. If you had the right combination of sails up, she would ride better than an ocean liner."

By the time Lieutenant-Commander Ken Brown took over her helm, the navy's longest-serving ship was long overdue for an ocean-racing win. In her next Vic-Maui Race, she found it.

"Second-place finish in the Victoria-Maui race has *Oriole's* skipper Brown chirping," trumpeted a July 8, 1990, newspaper headline. Lieutenant Larry Trim, navigator for that race, shared basking rights with a cadet crew from Royal Roads Military College, who were celebrating their school's 50th anniversary.

These photos, taken during the 1986 Vic-Maui race, show Oriole's *latticed spinnaker pole.*

Leading Seaman Pat O'Hara (left), who is repairing a sail, watch captain Doc Beaudry, and unidentified crewman are shown here during the 1986 Vic-Maui race. Beaudry spent a lot of time on the helm. "I had a habit of blowing out the mizzen staysail," he says. "We carried two, one very old, and we blew it out six times."

Oriole's winning strategy followed the square-rigger route down the coast to San Francisco, and then the Great Circle route west. "Ken Brown sails with bravado," says watch captain Steve Halliwell. "He let us push the boat."

Drama stalked the finish line. "I only had one man-overboard incident, but I nearly lost two at the same time," recalls Brown. "It was scary how fast a person's head disappears to stern when you are doing 12 knots." *Oriole* was running with full spinnaker, main, mizzen, and mizzen staysail. Astern was a U.S. Coast Guard ship, one of the welcoming boats.

The finish gun sounded, and Brown rounded up to drop the chute. The spinnaker pole came forward inside the guardrail, where the lee sheet flogs quite badly. One of the cadets hung on, and it flapped him right over the side. "I didn't even know he was overboard," says Brown. "I was looking back by the wheel and this head went by in the water, waving and yelling, 'I'm—okay—SIR!'"

The Man Overboard (MOB) alarm sounded. Larry Trim hurled the kisby ring over the side. Brown rounded up and stopped the ship. The spinnaker thrashed wildly in the total darkness. They got a GPS fix, but he was gone. "We did all the right things. Threw all our deck lights on. Went on to Channel 16 with MOB, MOB." The Coast Guard cutter also threw on its lights and spotted the sailor. "This great big guy with arms the size of my legs reached over the side and grabbed this scrawny little cadet with one arm and had him on board within about three minutes."

Oriole dropped anchor at Lahaina. Within two hours, the swimmer was back on board, just in time for the welcoming party. A few days later, the navy sailors played baseball with the Coast Guard rescuers. "They trounced us. We met the guy who fished him

1.5-ounce sailcloth or lighter. Brown made a stronger sail. "You could carry it in 30 knots of wind and just about pull the sticks out of her. That's one reason we did so well in 1990. We could fly that thing day and night, because it was 2.2-ounce cloth."

Ken Brown made two rigging changes to increase *Oriole*'s sail-handling efficiency. Frustration motivated the first. After an order to reduce sail using her traditional reef points took an hour and a half, Brown introduced "jiffy reefing." This method takes one minute and works with a cinch on the tack and clue. By cracking the halyard, the mainsail can be lowered significantly and then tacked back in at the clue with a stainless-steel bolt that lives in the track.

Lieutenant-Commander Ken Brown (above) campaigned HMCS Oriole *in a variety of overnight and long-distance races. Right: "Stokes" Steve Halliwell shows off a mahi mahi caught during the 1990 Vic-Maui race.*

out. We were just dead lucky," says Brown. "I don't know if we would ever have found him in that Molokai Strait with the sea running, maybe 20 knots of wind, trying to get sails squared away, and the engine going when it hadn't been running for days during the race."

An earlier incident had almost washed one of their two female crew members over the side in the same way. Her mates managed to keep her from going overboard. "It was their enthusiasm to get the sail down. They tried to control it. The small chute may have been up at the time, because I loved it," says Brown. Most spinnakers are made of

HMCS Oriole *celebrated her 70th anniversary with a dockside party in 1991.*

The other end uses a downhaul as a jigger, pulled aft and down.

Brown also rigged *Oriole* with a double headstay, so her headsails can be changed underway. This modification reduced the time to unhank the sail, hank on a new one, and rehoist. "So here's big *Oriole* with all that sail area, and she's suddenly got no headsail," explains Brown. "You have to pay off about 50 to 60 degrees off the wind. With the double headstay, if you are flying a big genoa, you hank on your smaller jib, run it up on the inside, and sheet it in. Now you have two headsails flying. You drop your big one, and the ship just keeps on going. You've now reduced your sail and could keep changing down until you got to a storm jib."

Cadets went up Vancouver Island's west coast on exercises to Bamfield, Ucluelet, and Tofino. "I could take them out and get them cold, wet, sick, and hungry, and bring them in every night and dry them out, and then take them out again the next day," says Brown. "After about the third day, they sort of got their sea legs."

Captain Brown was *Oriole*'s most experienced racing sailor. At the Maple Bay Yacht Club north of Victoria, he competed in many a regatta, in Moths, Snipes, Thunderbirds, and the elite northwest 6-Metre fleet. Brown entered *Oriole* in many overnight events. Three Oregon offshore Swiftsure feeder races that started at the Columbia River bar and ended in Victoria provided a good workup in optimum *Oriole* conditions: a close reach on a northwesterly. In the 1989 Southern Straits Race in the Gulf of Georgia, the wind died. In 1990, *Oriole* was one of the first yachts to round the Swiftsure mark before the dying wind left the boats drifting. She got home in two days.

A winter refit installed a new engine for a five-week Alaska training exercise in the summer of 1989. Tracy Arm, narrow and surrounded by steep rock, is too deep for a ship to anchor, so the crew sledge-hammered metal bars into a lumbering ice floe and secured *Oriole*'s lines to these spikes. They could almost step right off the deck onto this huge slab, which rose four feet above the water and resembled a floating parking lot. The men played baseball on the ice, and several cruising yachts took advantage of the makeshift mooring and rafted alongside for a sociable visit.

The assistant sail master, Leading Seaman Dave Greene, went to the top of the "stick" and marvelled at the overwhelming sense of solitude and grandeur.

Navigator Larry Trim took some men in the Zodiac to look at the glacier face. They barely escaped a direct hit when a big chunk calved off into the chuck. Says Brown, "That gave them a good ride." On the way home, a group of sea cadets boarded in Masset, Queen Charlotte Islands, and sailed to Queen Charlotte City.

In 1998, Trim and Greene returned to *Oriole* as captain and buffer. Their cook, Master Seaman Dale, was promoted to the prime minister's kitchen.

Ken Brown introduced a lasting legacy. "I used to call all my cooks 'Cookshack,'" he explains. "I started that on board *Oriole*. Cookshack one, two, three, four, five, six—I think I got up to Cookshack number 13. It's not a navy term. It was an old Cowichan Valley logging term that my dad used. He was a logger and a fisherman."

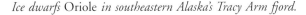

Ice dwarfs Oriole *in southeastern Alaska's Tracy Arm fjord.*

Bo Derek's Beach

*L*ieutenant-Commander Michael Cooper calls HMCS *Oriole* "the Canadian Forces recruiting poster." The Bedford, Nova Scotia, native transferred from an Ottawa desk to command *Oriole* in 1991 and circumnavigated Vancouver Island the next summer to commemorate the 125th anniversary of the Vancouver Island colony's confederation with the mainland. For the next two years, he expanded her community-relations programs and raised her international racing profile.

"A real love of the sea and a commitment to the navy is required to crew in her," he says. In 1993, the ship logged 145 days underway and travelled 11,366 nautical miles. Training cruises embarked regular army and reserve air force personnel from landlocked squadrons at Winnipeg, Manitoba; Yellowknife, Northwest Territories; and Moose Jaw, Saskatchewan.. The Royal Canadian Sea Cadet Corps Oriole came from Swan Hills, Alberta. The yacht achieved her best Swiftsure performance—second around the mark, finishing eighth overall—and won the Participation Trophy for having sailed in 38 races.

The "centre of hospitality" worked overtime. In 1993, nearly 1,000 guests boarded *Oriole* for day sails. Twenty-one public-relations events included season-opening ceremonies at the Seattle, Royal Victoria, and Royal Vancouver Yacht Clubs.

Receptions celebrated the retirement of Bill Walker's coxswain, Keith Hanna, who went on to head up the navy sea cadets in British Columbia. Guests came from the Bangor, Washington, submarine base, HMCS Discovery Vancouver reserve unit, 1st Garry Oak Sea Scouts, Powell River Sea Cadets, and five local high schools. The Victoria Symphony, Victoria Maritime Museum, and Paraplegic Society held charity auctions, offering a day-sail excursion in *Oriole* for the highest bidder.

Michael Cooper skippered *Oriole* for two ocean races. In 1993, she finished first in her Pacific Handicap Racing Fleet division and ninth overall in the 2,254-nm TransPac Race from Los Angeles to Honolulu. The next year, she entered the 1,300-nm San Diego-Manzanillo Race. The race started in the wake of a severe storm in a dying southwesterly, with shifting winds that hit almost every compass point during the first 24 hours. On the way down the coast, Cooper worked up his crew. Watches rotated seven hours on and five hours off. Junior cadets navigated, one on each watch. The women had their own space in the after cabins by the engine, but everyone moved off when the ship tied up for maintenance at the San Diego Yacht Club.

An *Oriole* job posting for a buffer/sail master position called for a petty officer, 2nd class. Ron

Ingalls was only a master seaman, but his credentials were solid. He competed for Canada at the 1991 World Military Sailing Championships in Pakistan. When Keith Hanna took over the base seamanship division, Ingalls replaced him as skipper of the Maritime Forces Pacific's only other sail-training yacht, the CS 36 *Goldcrest.* "Keith was the bosun trade rep. I checked with him, and he said no one else was interested [in the *Oriole's* buffer position]," says Ingalls. "It was a dream come true. I remember seeing *Oriole* when I was a sea cadet in Vancouver and thinking how great it would be to go sailing on board her. It was happening!"

Ingalls tells this dramatic story of the 1994 race from San Diego. "*Oriole* doesn't power well to weather, and we had started the race more than an hour late. Against the 30-knot southerly, she couldn't make more than 5 knots. Although the webbing in the bowsprit whiskers is usually secure, slamming into a wave jumped one of the girls right out of the safety net. The next swell washed her overboard. She was never scared, because we had practised this many times, so she was very confident there would be no problem and we would come back and pick her up.

"We raced to our Man Overboard stations. The engineer flashed up the engine. Some dived for the mast and crash-dropped the sails. We brought *Oriole* alongside the young lady, tossed the horseshoe flotation belt overboard, and hoisted her back using the mizzen staysail halyard. The only time she was hurt was swinging away from the ship and crashing back into the side. The *Oriole* is not that high off the water, and the exercise was over in about three minutes. She went below to warm up and was back on her next watch. At that time, we were in last place and radioed the other yachts that the girl was back on board. Now they are wondering if this really happened, or if we were just fooling them."

Oriole settled into the "slot," maintaining a 12-knot run, but slowed to 8 knots off Baja California. At midnight, each yacht called in to race headquarters. Three Santa Cruz 70s that had started two days after *Oriole* beat the navy ketch across the line. For the first time, Roy P. Disney was in charge of his dad's Santa Cruz 70 *Pyewacket.* With ace ocean racer Mark Rudiger as co-navigator, *Pye* carried an eight-man crew instead of the usual eleven, and a brand-new weather satellite system. She broke the elapsed-time record by six hours and finished twelve hours ahead of the next boat.

Mike Cooper understood how to maximize racing performance. He kept the ship light, removing extra water and fuel before competition. Normally, *Oriole* draws some eleven feet, but Cooper got her down to nine feet. "Tons came off that boat," says Ingalls. "We made fresh water from the reverse-osmosis machine and took spare parts off if we were near the base." As a result, *Oriole* had managed to hold on to first place in her division and race first overall until a manoeuvre to get up to the finish line near the beach dropped her to third overall.

The previous night, *Oriole* had started tacking toward the finish line off the isthmus where the Bo Derek movie *10* was filmed. The crew could see the powerboat that anchored one end of the line. But the other marker buoy wasn't lit, so in the darkness *Oriole* sailed toward the beach. "We saw the buoy go by on our port side, but it should have been on our starboard side, so we had to do a big swing around and do a whole circle and come back around up to the finish line," says Ingalls. "The line was so short that our bowsprit almost went through the committee boat. In light air against the wind, the huge headsail required everybody on board for the last critical yards. I used some of the useful tricks I learned from Doc Beaudry, like using *Oriole's* weight to 'shoot the mark.'"

Just before daylight, as soon as the navy ketch crossed the line, the crew flashed up the engine and readied the anchor to stop the boat from running up on the beach. The cox'n set off in the Zodiac to scope out where they could tie up. It was the first time this crew had moored Mediterranean style. They dropped the hook next to *Pyewacket*.

Ingalls continues, "The crew has been working solid since eight o'clock last night, and it's now about five o'clock in the morning. There is no way *Oriole* ever goes into port without looking pretty. After six days at sea, there's quite a few hours of work, like polishing brass, putting stuff away. The crew worked hard to get everything done. *Oriole* has no air conditioning, and it was muggy and hot below decks. By late afternoon, we were exhausted and looking for places to sleep. Some curled up on the beach. I got the bowsprit whiskers."

HMCS *Oriole* again topped her PHRF division and earned an unofficial title: "Sentimental Favourite."

In 1994, Michael Cooper was posted to Halifax, where he later skippered the Maritime Forces Atlantic's only sail-training yacht, a fibreglass CS 36 sloop called *Tuna II,* a sister ship to the Maritime Forces Pacific's sail-training vessel *Goldcrest.*

Cooper Sail Innovations

Mike Cooper wanted ideas for making *Oriole* go faster. Ron Ingalls recommended using the staysail. In very light air, the headsail pulls the bow down, and you end up using a lot of helm. The spinnaker staysail is hanked where you would normally use your headsail. "That light little sail takes shape in light air and gives pulling power," he says. "We used it off Baja as a ghoster to get underneath the 5-knot area."

Cooper also switched to full battened Kevlar/Dacron main and mizzen sails. They use special fibreglass "round type" battens in the luff area, so they will flex and not break, and "flat type" to give stiffness in the leech. Their advantages are the weight of the sail is reduced; it slides with less friction; there is less flogging; the sail life is extended; and the sail gets into shape sooner and is easier to fly. The disadvantages are that more care is needed when derigging, and they must be stored and cared for differently.

Cooper and Ingalls changed the track up the back of the masts to a Hacken Traveller system, including cars where the battens attach to the mast. "This has to be the longest traveller ever put together, says Ingalls. "The mainmast would have about 85 to 90 feet of track. But this made it so that *Oriole* only needs six to ten people to raise the main, versus the old way with fifteen to twenty."

SOUTH PACIFIC

Canada's Floating Ambassador

"*M*y dreams about a career in the Canadian navy and commanding *Oriole* all started after 1955, when my dad was posted to Esquimalt," says Lieutenant-Commander Michael Brooks. "I remember walking through the Dockyard when I was seven or eight and noticing this beautiful old sailing ship, the *Oriole*.

"My father gave me the inspiration to go and explore the world in a small way. First, building rafts on the shoreline of Esquimalt and exploring places like Brothers Island just off the entrance to the harbour. Then he pushed me off the beach in a kayak at Qualicum to paddle all day. When I went looking for our friends the Sweenys (he was a captain of *Oriole* later) amidst the large grey hulls in Esquimalt Harbour, we got a nasty call from the Queen's harbour master asking who that young idiot was out in the middle of the harbour in a plywood kayak. My dad had built it for me, and consequently got called onto the carpet of Admiral Rainer and reined in.

"I joined the navy in 1969 as a 'sparker' [communicator]. The illusion quickly disappeared as I was on my hands and knees in the flats of HMCS *Saskatchewan* scrubbing the decks and adhering to the routine of an ordinary seaman. But it was all good stuff that led to me advancing and knowing where to go in the navy. I went to university at St. Mary's, Halifax, to see if I could get myself caught up so I could be a commissioned officer and drive my own ship someday. In 1976, I was selected for officer training at NOTC Venture and navigated in HMCS *Gatineau, Chaleur,* and *Miramichi.* I left the navy in 1982 in Australia to pursue a lifelong dream of sailing tall ships.

"I found myself back in the navy in 1985, and after several more years at sea as a navigator, I started to focus on driving our 73-year-old naval sail-training ship that I remembered so well as a youth. I hooked up with Mike Cooper, who was the captain of the *Oriole* in 1992, did a couple of Swiftsures with him and a few trips off the west coast to Barkley Sound, and found myself flying to Hawaii to navigate her home from the 1992 TransPac race. At the end of that trip, Mike said, 'You are well and truly ready to be her commanding officer.' I was excited and elated at the opportunity of taking the helm. In 1994 I assumed command, after a very quick turnover. I was given this awesome responsibility, not only to represent the government, but to train young people in our maritime heritage. I found myself facing challenges every day."

Three months after Lieutenant-Commander Michael Brooks took command in May 1994, HMCS *Oriole* basked in the XV Commonwealth Games spotlight. Berthed in front of Victoria's Empress Hotel from August 14 to 19, 1994, Canada's floating embassy hosted a round of receptions.

Heading the August 18 entries in *Oriole*'s guest book, scrawled halfway down the page, is the signature EDWARD. The auspicious outing began when Admiral Richard Waller escorted His Royal Highness Prince Edward, Earl of Wessex, past the Small Boat Unit's grey YAGs to the gleaming white ketch. Before the prince's day cruise, security was tight; a navy diving team searched the hull for explosives, while RCMP officers observed with binoculars from Signal Hill. Other undercover officers mingled with the invited guests. The RCMP *Nadon* patrolled off Victoria Harbour.

The light-blue royal standard fluttered as *Oriole* ghosted along the Victoria waterfront. "Prince

Edward's a sailor and took the helm a lot of the time. He really enjoyed the boat and how balanced she was," says Brooks. "I was bragging about how impressed I am with the way *Oriole* handles. Just like a dinghy. Very fast to respond. During his time on board it was as though he wasn't royalty. He was very frank and just a very nice guy. It was fun."

"The *Oriole* is Canada's most cost-effective ambassador," says Malcolm Anderson, whose brother, David, was the federal minister of revenue at the time of the Games. The Andersons' great-great grandfather, Victoria businessman J. H. Todd, led the lobby that established the nineteenth-century Royal Navy graving dock hard by *Oriole*'s jetty. David Anderson took his Australian Games guests day-sailing in *Oriole*.

When her primary role as a sail-training ship is combined with international good-will missions, *Oriole* is a cost-effective ambassador. But the ship also has fans who know her by reputation only. The world often arrives in envelopes postmarked Malta, or Britain, asking for souvenirs like the ship's crest. One thank-you letter ends "… many times as a young man I would be out beating towards Race Rocks in an old 15 ft. Snipe. Whenever I spotted the *Oriole* heaving under full canvas, I would immediately slip into daydreaming …"

"My four years in *Oriole* were absolutely phenomenal," comments Brooks, "as I allowed myself to be directly involved with the technology of sailing and how it had progressed up until 1921 when she was launched, and how it really hasn't advanced that much in physics from that particular time. It's the lightweight materials that obviously make the difference. *Oriole* was a stallion in her time, fast and capable. Every day presented a new vision of what it was like to have sailed in the grand old days of tall ships. Every day brought a lesson … I found myself in the 1996 Vic-Maui race, for instance, off the coast

"The admiral introduced [Prince Edward] to me on the jetty," says Michael Brooks, "and I escorted him onto the ship. In royal protocol, the Queen gets a 'pipe.' Her family [doesn't]. But if I accompany him across the brow, then they pipe him. He stood at attention and then he shook hands with everybody. We had a buffet laid on of soup and sandwiches and of course various other delightful snacks. Admiral Waller loaned us his steward and staff to help."

of Oregon, stuck, becalmed, not going anywhere, but drifting with the tide for four days. I learned very quickly what it was like not only just sailing in heavy weather and racing, but to coax a 92-ton ship along and eventually use apparent wind to lift her up and get her going even when there is no true wind to be had. It was like dinghy sailing, inducing heel in light air, getting the sails full, not using the rudder, of course, but coaxing her along to look for a little puff of wind, so that eventually she would sail on her own. That's what won the Sydney-Hobart Race in 1997— the skill of sailing in no wind.

"Captain Foldessi, who at that time was naval attaché to the Australian government, initiated the invitation in a letter to Admiral Bruce Johnstone for *Oriole* to take part in the 200th anniversary of Bass and Flinders' circumnavigation of Tasmania. So I set to planning a journey that would take advantage of the shifting highs and lows of the Pacific, and the currents in the tropical convergence zone and the trades, and found the ideal time to make it down and back in seven short months. Commodore Ronald Buck and Admiral Russ Moore gave their stamp of approval."

On October 14, 1997, HMCS *Oriole*'s helm quivered in his hand as Brooks pointed her bow into the prevailing westerly, outward bound on a 7,550-nm South Pacific good-will tour. Over the next seven months, Canada's floating ambassador "showed the flag" at San Francisco, Pearl Harbor, Palmyra, Kiribati, Western Samoa, Fiji, New Caledonia, Australia, New Zealand, Tahiti, and Christmas Island.

"We set off with a group of people who had been transferred over to the navy from other occupations," Brooks recalls, "and soon found them enjoying the challenge of sail training after a very rough and heavy sea to San Francisco, where we lost three people to sea sickness, including the cook, and spent five days alongside to allow ourselves to regroup for the long journey across to Hawaii to Pearl Harbor. We arrived in Pearl Harbor on the 7th of November after shooting through the Molokai Express, a wind/sea combination that blows between Maui and Molokai Island. Lahaina is just down below the isthmus that extends northeast where everybody goes to anchor. Sail ten minutes northwest to Molokai, and you are hit with this huge funnel of air that comes down with the combination of hot air rising off the islands with the trades that are coming across from San Francisco. On several occasions, 25- and 30-foot seas laid *Oriole* on her side. People speak of Bass Strait, the dreaded Tasman Sea, but it can get pretty ugly just off the coast here, as well as in Hawaii.

"That brought us to Pearl Harbor going down to this very, very narrow channel where it gets ugly year-round. As the high moves down specifically at that time of the year, when we were there, we had to go further south to make the trans-Pacific break. At Pearl Harbor, we got ready for the next leg of the journey.

"We were treated royally at Pearl Harbor. We were given a berth right in front of the admiral's

Lieutenant-Commander Michael Brooks commanded HMCS Oriole*'s only tour to the southern latitudes.*

office. He made a habit of coming down on a regular basis to see how we were making out and set up a briefing scenario with meteorological research for me; an ideal routing for the boat; taking her down; taking advantage of the winds. Then the captain of the meteorological and typhoon storm-watch centre at Pearl Harbor set up an incredible Power Point briefing and everything else. At the end of it, the captain gave me a crest made out of particleboard and wished us fair winds and following seas. This crest hung in my cabin proudly as I every day downloaded, using [satellite communications system] Inmarsat Charlie, all the latest weather pictures, warnings of containers that had gone adrift, last sightings, and all these problems that can go bump in the night. I would get these weathers downloaded from the United States Navy in conjunction with Canadian Hydrographic Service Office in Esquimalt, as well as utilizing my Internet link with Captain Bob's weather centre in Hawaii, where you get a picture of the whole North Pacific.

"We found ourselves sailing basically downhill all the way to Sydney, Australia. Everything was either on our side or on our back. It was just phenomenal. I carried a couple of extra fuel tanks to get us across the equator, because of the intertropical conversion zone. But because of El Niño and all the weather systems shifting farther to the south, we virtually sailed right across the tropical conversion zone hardly ever using the engines.

"Our trip from Pearl Harbor took us down to Palmyra atoll, which is a privately owned American place and absolutely gorgeous. A big huge lagoon with sharks clearly visible from 50 feet of water. The students got the opportunity to swing from vines from palm trees and splash into the lagoon. From there we went on to Kanton in the Phoenix Group, which, incidentally, was the satellite-tracking station for the [early mannedspace flights]. All the equipment has been left. The tarmac, the airport, all the married quarters for the United States airmen, including the huge satellite-tracking radars which had just been left there to rot, and the rebar is all rusty. The kids from the Kiribas Nation who inhabit the island are just playing in amongst all this garbage. It was quite a sad sight to see, but the Americans, as in the case of Palmyra, are making an extremely pointed effort to clean up the islands. The Seebees were in at Palmyra when I was there to clean up the old runway and get rid of the garbage, so there is a move afoot to get with it. From there we sailed to Western Samoa, enjoyed another couple of days alongside, and then on to Suva, Fiji. I actually met the commanders that overthrew the government the following year.

"Probably the most intriguing island to visit in the South Pacific was New Caledonia. Nouméa is still a French protectorate. In there I met with the admiral of the South Pacific fleet. The French have a very strong affinity to the welfare of the South Pacific. A lot of it is French territory that I wasn't really aware of before. The officer cadets in particular enjoyed a grand lunch put on by the admiral. There was a white awning, white-gloved servants who are native people. It was like looking back to the '20s when *Oriole* was in her heyday. We sailed into Sydney Harbour on the 19th of December 1997 with a brand-new 2.5-ounce gennaker that was specifically made for the trip by North Sails. Emblazoned in the middle was a crest of *Oriole*. It made me very proud to sail in through the Heads."

Southerly
Busters

Stately windjammers gathered on January 19, 1998, for the Southern Hemisphere's largest tall ships gathering since the 1988 Australia bicentennial. Bristling with spars, Sydney's Darling Harbour showcased the fleet. The official host ship, *Young Endeavour,* was Britain's bicentennial gift to her former island colony. Square-rigged ships dazzled dock walkers: Russia's *Palada* and *Nadezhda,* the Mexican navy barque *Cuauhtemoc,* Indonesia's officer sail-training barquentine *Dewa Ruci,* and the British brigantine *Eye of the Wind.*

"It was appropriate for Canada to attend," says Michael Brooks, "since we share a common maritime heritage with Australia through the explorers Captain Cook and Captain Vancouver. I felt so proud to fly the Canadian flag in our beloved *Oriole* so far from home. Just by our very presence, I believe we showed those not familiar with our country, especially those sailors of the western Pacific, that our nation is serious about our maritime history and our shared concern for the oceans of the world. By the outcome of the race, we would hit that point home far more than we had bargained for."

In January 1998, below the bridge by Sydney's maritime museum, *Oriole* buzzed with last-minute preparations for the 750-nm Sydney-Hobart Tall Ships Race. Lieutenant Larry Trim flew to Sydney to replace Lieutenant-Commander Scott Crawshaw as executive officer. The next four months served as Trim's orientation before he took over as captain in June. The first group of NOTC cadets flew back to Victoria and was replaced by eleven classmates. The new crew had time for only a few practice day sails to learn about running backstays, jiggers, blocks, and bowlines.

They were excited, but apprehensive. They had heard about the "southerly busters"—huge fronts that boil up from the bottom of the world, whiz through the Bass Strait, and sweep across the Tasman Sea. Winds that blow up rapidly from calm to gale. Winds that change direction 50 degrees and slap you in the face. Winds that punch survival buttons.

On Australia Day, January 26, it seemed as if all mayhem had broken loose in Darling Harbour. A scorching sun seared the thousands of people who lined the shore to watch the floating scrum. Hundreds of small boats churned long white wakes as they escorted the tall ships parade. Stopping them from darting under the bowsprit caused anxious moments on *Oriole*'s foredeck. Choppers carrying television camera crews constantly hovered mere feet in front of her vulnerable headstay. Royal Australian Airforce jets screamed overhead in tight formation. "Criss-crossing powerboats with jolly blokes at the helm and their 'sheilas' hanging over the stern were a real entertainment for all the crews," says Brooks. "What a party!"

The Parade of Sail wound deep around Kangaroo Island, out through the narrows under the Sydney Harbour Bridge, and past the Sydney Opera House. *Oriole* maintained her place in the line and paid her respects to VIPs aboard the saluting ship HMAS *Hobart*, anchored just off the naval dockyard Woolloomooloo. A left turn off Port Jackson and a right turn out the Heads brought the fleet into the Pacific Ocean.

As the wind freshened to 25 knots, Brooks toyed with the idea of hoisting full sail for a magnificent photo shoot. But sea room was tight. "I opted out, and a good thing too," he says. "*Cuauhtemoc* hoisted in the tight waters astern, and it wasn't long before she got into trouble. My heart went thunk when I heard the crunch as she careened off Kangaroo Island. My pilot's radio was alive with panic from race officials and the pilotage authority. Luckily, there was no major damage."

For this trip, as a safety measure, a new chart table had been built beside the mizzenmast, enabling the helmsman to consult the chart without leaving the wheel. Previously, the coachhouse roof had doubled as a chart table. Several years before Brooks' command, luck had prevented a serious accident when the main boom topping lift parted and sent the heavy spar crashing down, narrowly missing the navigator.

HMCS Oriole *is seen here in January 1998, with the Sydney Harbour Bridge as a backdrop.*

Fifty-two boats milled around the starting line for the Sydney-Hobart Race. The first gun sent off 36 small C Class yachts; the next sent the tall ships. Down the coast, *Oriole* stood a little offshore to get better winds. The 300-foot *Palada* and 270-foot *Cuauhtemoc* sailed a parallel course 200 nautical miles to port of the ketch. The square-riggers had to battle the westerlies back to Tasmania, while *Oriole* used them to her advantage to crimp back into the coast.

Australian television cameramen travelled on board four glamour boats. Their cameos showed *Young Endeavour* crew playing deck games, and

Palada trainees at long tables, hunched over math, astronomy, and science lessons while their captain jogged laps around the deck. On board *Oriole*, Ben Davies filmed accidental strawberry-jam middens and the crew's first hot meal in three days—steak.

Oriole army medic Brad Olmstead called the weather conditions "Down and dirty, like Whitbread racing." Twice a day, the captain's laptop cranked out forecasts from Esquimalt. The weather got very ugly, very fast. On the southern horizon, an ominous storm cloud hung like an enormous anvil, marking the place where the Indian Ocean air and water hit the hot Australian coast. The resulting winds give the Sydney-Hobart race its notoriety. (The next year, several racers drowned.)

As the cloud loomed closer, Brooks considered tucking in to Eden, a small town on Australia's southeast tip and the last anchorage before the Bass Strait. "I decided I would make a run for it and see if I could take advantage of it, because I didn't believe, and no one had indicated to us, that there were winds that strong. Australians don't have 24-hour marine broadcasts like ours." Every day, *Oriole* broadcast the weather conditions to the other boats. Ships carrying younger crew who had to go aloft to furl the sails were especially glad to get this information.

Lines flailed. Crew started to bruise. Brooks flashed up the engine, backtracked, and radioed the rest of the fleet. Many smaller sailboats followed *Oriole* into Eden and anchored. The wind dropped to a steady 35 to 40 knots and veered to give them a better angle for the direct "lay line" to Hobart.

By this time, the inevitable rivalries had developed. *Palada* emerged as the boat to beat. *Cuauhtemoc* resorted to match-racing tactics (as seen in America's Cup competition) to sneak past the Russians, and headed out to sea. The Mexicans controlled their manoeuvres and sail changes with an intricate series of whistles that probably confused the escorting albatross.

For most of the race, *Oriole* sailed rail down. "If you missed a few spokes on the wheel or misjudged a wave, the result would be many tons of water sweeping the deck," says Larry Trim. One wave broke over the beam, cascaded like a waterfall down the companionway and into the wardroom, and seeped into the bilge. The wind destroyed one spinnaker and tore a headsail. Short, violent seas fractured the pulpit.

Men who could handle steering in heavy weather—Michael Brooks, Larry Trim, Cox'n Peter LeBlanc, and Buffer Stu Jackman—took frequent breaks during long hours at the helm. Once, Trim went for a "swim" above the deck. On the leeward side of the wheel, up to his armpits in water, he was trying to steer around the back of a wave when another chest-high wave knocked him off his feet. After floating horizontally for a few seconds, he fell to the deck and crawled on his hands and knees back to the helm. "We stayed wet for seven days," he says.

Larry Trim had logged more than 10,000 offshore miles in warships. But the "busters" were worse than any other weather he remembers. He admits to being a little nervous. "But *Oriole* is so seaworthy. I was more scared for the crew, inexperienced people who didn't have their sea legs. A lot of them were wide-eyed the whole time."

Three years later, in the Naden wardroom on Signal Hill's southern slope, a cadet who survived the wrath of the "busters," Lieutenant Chris McKelvey of HMCS *Algonquin*, shares vivid memories of that trip. LeBlanc and Jackman had divided the cadets into two groups, which stood six-hour watches during the day and four hours during the night. "Some did not want to come up on watch because they were terrified," says McKelvey, "but that's your job. It's not like somebody saying, 'Get up on deck right now.' You're down there sleeping. You're woken up for your watch and you know you have to relieve somebody else up on deck."

On watch, the trainees clipped themselves to the boat with safety harnesses. Powerful walls of water often knocked the tethered tars clear across the foredeck. McKelvey wasn't terrified, but admits to some nervous moments, "especially after I went swinging over the ocean and just about ended up in the water in the middle of the dark. I didn't think that anyone could come and get me. There were sharks out there."

Tremendous seas taxed the crew. Many times they worked the sails while sea water washed over their heads. In rough weather, one of the spinnaker booms kept popping out. Around three in the morning, the Yankee sail got wrapped around it. "That was quite exciting, as we were right in the middle of those 25-foot seas, trying to pull that stuff back in," says navigator Stan Wedell, who was strapped in at the bow as the swell poured over the bowsprit. "You couldn't take a breath if you were trying to pull in the spinnaker boom. You are so focussed on trying to get the job done. You just want to get the equipment repaired and back together, because you know everybody else depends on you."

By the sixth day, the seas had flattened enough for more video filming. Nattily attired in navy blue trousers and middy tops, the *Palada* crew stood at attention to pay their ritual respects to the flag and the sea. The *Oriole* crew patched her spinnaker. Within a few hours, she was becalmed at the mouth of the Derwent River. As an outflow current set her slowly backward, the great bird in the centre of her "kite" drooped.

Cuauhtemoc was doubling as a little piece of Mexico sailing around the world. There was plenty to keep her crew from getting homesick. The video camera captured ebullient musicians jauntily dressed in blue-and-white striped T-shirts. "No wind today. This bad for sailing, but very good for picnic," said the mate, as cooks shuttled steaming trays to the upper deck, where a portable taco bar supported a feast.

A chorus of horns and shouts greeted HMCS *Oriole* as she drifted over the Hobart Harbour finish line, first of the tall ships. "We were trying to fill the sails with muscle," commented one sailor. "The only thing that got us across that line was sheer persistence." On *Arung Samudera*, the Indonesians danced and sang their way to second place. Coming in third, the *Young Endeavour* crew was content to beat *Palada*. Partying as they crossed the line, the *Chuauhtemoc* crew finished fourth.

This was also a special year for Tasmania. Two centuries had passed since the explorers George Bass and Matthew Flinders discovered that the continent's southeastern tip was an island. Departing in a 36-foot boat from Sydney, some 800 nautical miles to the north, the pair circumnavigated what was then known as Van Diemen's Land. Hobart was celebrating this maritime heritage when the tall ships tied up. In full carnival mode, Bass Flinders Bicentennial Maritime Festival celebrants flocked to Hobart's harbourside. At the prize-giving in St. David's Park, *Oriole* collected four trophies: the first tall ship across the line, the fastest time in 24 hours for the Eden-Hobart run, excellence in communication for informing everyone about the weather, and sailing the longest distance to participate.

The Kiwi Connection

*H*omeward-bound, HMCS *Oriole* crossed the Tasman Sea to Nelson, on the northwestern tip of New Zealand's South Island, where I joined her for the Kiwi leg of her voyage. Along the Cook Strait's southern shore, the Marlborough Sounds plunge fjords deep into the roof of New Zealand's South Island. As we power toward Picton on February 22, 1998, Michael Brooks conducts "church parade" on the foredeck. This brief worship service maintains the *Oriole II* tradition reported in her log records: "Sunday devotions took place after breakfast, with slow-time banjo accompaniment by the professor."

As we enter Picton's compact harbour, a pungent odour assaults our nostrils. Piles of donated cattle feed ferment on the dock. Behind the rolling mountains, Marlborough County's parched pastures deliver a cargo that moos its way into the freighter berthed on the other side of our pier. All over New Zealand, El Niño is sending this year's undersized cattle and sheep prematurely to slaughter.

Two days later, while most of my shipmates enjoy shore leave in this picture-postcard port, I am on board with the duty watch. In the wardroom, John "Cookshack" Manley lifts a section of the oiled teak wardroom deck. Reaching into the freezer, he pulls out dinner: steak and yet another pan of Tasmanian cheesecake. In Wellington, he will replace two broken electric frying pans and an electric crockpot. Cadet MacKenzie writes postcards. Cadet Snow works on the small plaques that will be presented to dignitaries when *Oriole* represents Canada at the week-long Wellington International Festival of the Arts. He meticulously outlines tiny gold feet and the outside gold ring on the bird crests—an eight-hour job.

0530, February 25. The aroma of frying bacon fills what Keith Hanna calls the "cave" and Scott Crawshaw calls the "tissue box"—the "rack" where I sleep, which is concealed by blue curtains behind the wardroom port settee. The crew sifts down the companionway. Iana Fisher, our only female trainee, arrives and disappears into the coxswain's cabin. She returns in navy slacks, carrying her off-duty blue jeans, and stows them in the top half of our double bunk. "What, no muffins?" She shakes a "seasick" pill out of the communal bottle on the sideboard and washes it down with a glass of milk. Cadet Terryberry clatters down the companionway. "Ah, coffee!" Adjusting his black beret, he carries his mug backup to his morning watch on the chilly deck.

Today's forecast warns of a high-pressure system moving east. On the starboard settee, Cadet Bader pulls on sea boots and wetskins and announces to no one in particular, "We had Joel say a little prayer.

In the pilotage for the *World Notice to Mariners,* there are two bad straits in this part of the world. We've been through one. Guess what's the other?" The Cook Strait funnels between mountains that flank the North and South Islands. In this volatile stretch of water, the wind can whip up from nothing to 100 knots. Yesterday's gale kept the fast ferry *Lynx* docked across from *Oriole.*

Buffer Stu Jackman joined the navy after Sea Scouts in Winnipeg and spent fourteen of the next sixteen years at sea. On this trip, he has brought his wetsuit and scuba gear so that he can check the transducer, propeller, and other areas of the hull for damage. Today, he quarterbacks the departure action.

0800. The engine kicks into slow-throb mode. Buff paces up and down the deck, shouting the signals that will lob us into the path of the predicted front. "Standby lines and fenders. Let's go! Heave in on one. Heave in on four. Check two. Check three. Hold three. Down slack three. Fend off."

LeBlanc expertly jockeys the grey Zodiac and nudges *Oriole*'s bow slowly away from the jetty. "Stand by to recover the zode."

As we power over a pale turquoise mirror, a rosy glow suffuses the rounded hills. Larry Trim steers while Michael Brooks finishes his coffee. Navigating Officer Hamish Thom wipes dew off the chart table. Their rubber-soled sandals squidge as the bare-legged cadets mop the bowsprit with paper towels, hose down the decks, and scrub them with Turk's-heads on long handles. *Oriole* rolls gently as the *Lynx* scuds by. In less than three hours she will be in Wellington. It will take us half the day to travel the 80 kilometres.

1100. A refreshing breeze tugs at *Oriole*'s rigging as the fjord fans out into the Cook Strait. Bull kelp drifts by, reminding me of Victoria's Brotchie Ledge. The lookout scans the building chop, alert for drifting logs. Bagged on the foredeck,

the jib is shackled to the halyard, ready to hoist along the headstay. Along the main boom, the royal-blue sail cover waits to be untied and whisked off. Another shackled halyard readies the mainsail headboard to feed into the mainmast track.

Pulling on wetskin pants, the trainees head for their tacking stations. Brooks yells, "C'mon. We haven't got all day. Let's get those headsails up." All hands rally to hoist the main, mizzen, Yankee, and jumbo. Trim steadies the wheel on a northeast course for the entrance to Wellington Harbour. Whitecaps riffle the pale-green strait as the wind builds, pressuring *Oriole* on a broad reach toward the mouth of the harbour. Engineer Murray "Stokes" Panagrot cuts the engine. Orders fly. "Get the main sheet right out. We can carry more foresail. Stand by the gennaker."

1130. "How's she feel?" Brooks asks the helmsman. "Still not a good enough angle. Bring her up and point for that land, please. Okay. That's a good heading right there." The starboard watch is sent below to eat. In the galley, we take turns concocting our own sandwiches from platters of sliced ham, beef, and turkey. "Do not, anybody, open the refrigerator up, please and thank you," says Cookshack. A coffee urn bursts its lashing, crashing onto the wardroom floor.

At noon, Brooks orders everyone to the high side. Trim is still steering. At the chart table, Cadet Underhill wields an eraser and orange wax pencil, correcting the tracks he plotted in Picton. Cadets Kam, Wall, Freeman, and Landstrom crouch along the high side, polishing brass. Our acting sub-lieutenants are already dreaming about their final exercise to Alaska in the "sweeps"—the mahogany-hulled minesweepers—where they will be warm and dry.

1240. As we round up outside the reef at the entrance to Wellington Harbour, half a dozen small

Navigating officer Hamish Thom, trainee Iana Fisher, and Michael Brooks at the chart table on the Oriole *bridge in New Zealand's Marlborough Sounds.*

Officer cadets hoist sail in Marlborough Sounds.

sailboats play tag. "Takedown, you guys," orders Brooks. "Nice. Let's get it bagged." Someone mutters, "There's that bloody *Lynx*. She's already been there and back." Twenty minutes later, we tie up at the Port of Wellington pier, where Ian Price gives us a hand with the lines. Price is the ship's New Zealand gopher, troubleshooter, and logistics helper. "What happened?" he asks. "We didn't expect you until four o'clock!"

Wednesday, March 6, 0600. The generator's gentle vibration announces breakfast. Cookshack has heaped the wardroom sideboard with bananas, peaches, honeydew, bagels, yogurt, and fresh fruit salad for the new crew. Another milestone is happening: HMCS *Oriole*'s first rotation of non-Canadian trainees has replaced the Venture crew. There are five Australians and five New Zealanders. Four are female.

0700. As the streetlights flick off, cars snake around the capital city's long shoreline. Two artifacts from last week's official mission have found a berth in the commanding officer's head: an iron stowed by the porthole, and a pair of polished black shoes. A Brisbane trainee stands morning watch. Last night, Cookshack had first watch. "It's been a long night," he comments as he goes ashore for a last shower.

The core crew straggles back. Electrician Eric "Fish" Poisson, engineer Murray "Stokes" Panagrot, and foredeck man Doug Sanders arrive together and disappear down the aft hatch. At the chart table, Larry Trim eats a pastry and checks the tracks that will navigate us around the "dog-leg" crook in Wellington's long harbour. Sail bags nestle on the starboard foredeck. The gennaker is sausaged and tied at intervals.

Hair pulled back and braided, two Aussie midshipmen fold the mizzen and mainsail covers. As the trainees scrub the deck, the *Lynx* rooster-tails toward the strait. Brooks has traded his whites

Seated on the spreaders, medic Brad Olmstead repairs the GPS antenna in Wellington, New Zealand.

for navy shorts and a blue shirt. I slather Pre-Sun 29 for sensitive skin over my face and hope for the best. Half a dozen dolphins escort us toward the open water. "It's neat when they come up and rub their bellies against the hull," says Peter LeBlanc, who is a 28-year navy veteran.

New Zealanders are devout mariners. They put sailboats on postage stamps and revere solo sailor Sir Francis Chichester. Last week, hourly newscasts updated the positions of the approaching Whitbread Around-the-World racing yachts. We are travelling toward the 180th meridian, the invisible boundary that divides yesterday from today. I've been warned about the notorious strip between Wellington and Gisborne, where we are headed. "It's a shit piece of water, very similar to the Capetown to Natal stretch," one sailor told me in a local café. "Every time we went to Gizzie, we got a pasting. We tried to hug the coast and still got lambasted. It was bloody uncomfortable."

Telescoped along the deck, the trainees wait to practise the drills they rehearsed dockside at Wellington. Buffer's commands boom, "When I say 'two and six,' everybody lean forward; when I say 'heave,' everybody lean back. Keep your heads down and inboard. Pretty soon, you'll understand why. Pull together."

1315. White puffs wreathe the pale cliffs to port as we power toward the Pacific Ocean. One of the women steers. Another stretches out on the deck. An officer advises, "You had better not lie there. You'll get stepped on." Over coffee around the wardroom table, the Australian tri-service women describe how they were selected. Seventy applicants wrote an essay on values. Their commander evaluated their final ten-minute oral tests and chose our three trainees.

The young women still have to be boat-trained. One opens her cosmetics bag, pulls out a comb, and squirts hairspray. I escape up the companionway and find *Oriole*'s bow splitting the swells. Spray spumes over the foredeck and boils down the scuppers. In Wellington, Larry Trim replaced the aging yellow wet-weather suits with Musto offshore gear. Still wearing their navy shorts, the trainees cluster around the bridge in their white, red, and chartreuse jackets, looking like exotic tropical birds.

By late afternoon, mobile objects are secured in anticipation of the front. The red-crowned ensign staff that usually stows beside the companionway is lashed under the wardroom skylight. The brass binnacle-cover wedges between the commanding officer's head and the steel bulkhead. *Oriole* hobby-horses through the chop toward the North Island's most southeasterly cape, named after Admiral Hugh Palliser, who published Captain Cook's first charts. The deck watch wriggle into their new red wetskin pants and fasten their safety harnesses.

As we alter course to the north, Trim goes below for new charts. The core crew is alert to subtle changes in the rigging that go unnoticed by the new arrivals. Stokes sprints to adjust the tension on the backstay that supports the mainmast. Fish races to back him up. A new wind slams *Oriole* on the nose. An unanchored cap flies overboard, followed by a package of cookies from the deck and papers from the bridge. Everywhere, bodies lean over the guardrails. Buffer's boots suction along the slanting deck as he paces back and forth bellowing, "Pay attention to me. Hoist! Get those sails up!"

In the wardroom, unanchored chairs slide across the floor. I sit down hard on one and feel the leg collapse under me. Doc consoles, "It wouldn't be the first time." The storm slowly subsides into an apricot sunset that backlights the black hills as we glide across a molten sea. Several albatross befriend us and wheel lazily alongside. One of the women comes up the companionway and is immediately reprimanded: "Don't be caught with a toothbrush in your mouth. Hold on to something."

Thursday, March 6, 0700. The weather fax spits out news of a huge weather system coming in from the south. "I wish we had left Wellington at eight rather than ten," says the captain. The Yankee and jumbo balance *Oriole* comfortably, but we have to keep to the schedule planned a year ago in Canada, so we can't crack off for an exhilarating rail-down tack out to sea. Stokes has been tracking news faxes from the Nagano Winter Olympic Games and reports that Canadian hockey star Paul Kariya could be out for the season.

"Cleaning stations" in Napier, New Zealand. A Kiwi trainee polishes brass before HMCS Oriole *embarks on her homeward voyage.*

1700. A cadet logs our position on a notepad on top of the chart. GPS fix: 39°40° south latitude, 177° east longitude. *Oriole* closes Cape Kidnappers, which Cook named when Maoris tried to make off with his cabin boy. The headland intercepts the ocean surge, churning plankton to the surface. This interaction supports a major tourist attraction: 13,000 gannets in three colonies. Ahead, a line of dark spikes pokes through the haze—Napier's famous Norfolk pines.

It is a challenging harbour entrance—misty and right into the sun—for Trim, who is navigating. "I couldn't see any of the nav aids," he says. "The GPS lined us up." I ask him about the thump that woke me on Wednesday night. "We went through one wave and down the next," he explains. "We knew it

was there. We hit swells up to three metres." As *Oriole* heads toward the cement silos of Napier's man-made port, the sandy bluff reminds the captain of a familiar Juan de Fuca landmark: "This looks like Port Townsend."

Napier and Victoria are "twin cities." Michael Brooks performs his last official New Zealand duty and delivers a letter and gift—Lynn Milnes' book *In a Victoria Garden*—from Victoria's mayor to his Kiwi counterpart. In "scorchio" heat, I trudge along the waterfront for a last visit with the crew. Some trainees are polishing brass; others are preparing *Oriole* for the three-month journey back to British Columbia. Chiselled into the New Napier Arch in the art deco seaside promenade, an epigram reminds me of my shipboard experience: COURAGE IS THE THING: ALL GOES IF COURAGE GOES.

After *Oriole* left New Zealand, a tropical depression generated horrendous weather, and she punched into big seas from Tahiti to Christmas Island. In Hawaii, two Victoria reporters joined the crew. Armed with notepad, tape recorder, and camera, Susan Down filed her first Victoria *Times Colonist* story from a Pearl Harbor Internet cafe. One tale relates the trials of a mid-floor drain where water sloshes according to the angle of heel. "Someone posted a humorous sign stating that anyone wanting a shower should ask the captain to change tack." Rob Germain documented the passage for Victoria's CHEK-TV.

By the time HMCS *Oriole* sailed past Cape Flattery in May 1998 and entered the Juan de Fuca Strait on the final leg of her South Pacific saga, Michael Brooks had logged the longest voyage of any commanding officer. A thorough inspection of her hull, rigging, and gear occupied the next few months. As a result, she missed the Swiftsure that year, one of only a few times in her West Coast career when she wasn't on the starting line.

Members of a Winnipeg squadron shoulder HMCS Oriole's spinnaker pole during a 1999 pre-Swiftsure crew workup (top) and do a balancing act during the windless start of the race.

Friendship
Through Sport

*L*arry Trim, HMCS *Oriole*'s youngest commanding officer, was 36 years old when he took over from Michael Brooks in June 1998. Trim was born in London, England, grew up in Victoria, and entered the navy through HMCS *Malahat* Reserve Division. He joined the regular force in 1986 and completed the Destroyer Navigating Officer course. At the time of his posting to *Oriole,* Trim was combat officer in HMCS *Fredericton* on NATO patrol in Europe.

Trim rates sailing in "southerly buster" conditions as the highlight of his seventeen months on the *Oriole* bridge. Closer to home, he took great satisfaction in taking people on day sails around the Victoria waterfront, showing them how majestic a vessel *Oriole* is. When Trim left the ship in August 1999 to earn his bachelor of commerce at Royal Roads University, Scott Crawshaw replaced him as captain.

In 2000, Lieutenant-Commander Larry Trim returned to Esquimalt Harbour to chair the Maritime Forces Pacific committee that mounted the Conseil International du Sport Militaire's (CISM) annual world military sailing championship. CISM was created in 1948 to foster "friendship through sport." By bringing together on the playing field warriors who might formerly have settled their national differences with guns, CISM aims to promote world peace. Its 122 member nations form one of the world's

largest multidisciplinary organizations; its infrastructure ranks second only to that of the International Olympic Committee.

The championship was hosted by the Canadian Forces Sailing Association (CFSA) at its newly upgraded waterfront facilities during the first week of June 2001. Once again, the Naden Band of Maritime Forces Pacific continued its longstanding association with waterfront activities, performing at CISM ceremonies and social events for the Chiefs of Mission and teams from fifteen nations. Once again, shouts of "starboard" reverberated along the Esquimalt waterfront as these elite international sailors jostled for room at the mark and crossed tacks. Once again, an *Oriole* yacht doubled as an international centre of hospitality, as Lieutenant-Commander Scott Crawshaw welcomed visitors from Finland, Italy, the United States, France, Sweden, Spain, Norway, the Netherlands, Denmark, Chile, Poland, Belgium, Turkey, and South Africa on board Canada's "floating embassy" during the week of *Oriole*'s 80th birthday.

Vice-Admiral Ronald D. Buck summed it up best. "On this, the occasion of her 80th birthday, I think it's important to reflect on what HMCS *Oriole* represents. *Oriole* represents the history of the navy. She represents the heart and soul of the navy in the sense that while technology moves onward and we

Larry Trim steers HMCS Oriole *out of Victoria Harbour for a day of crew workups before the 1999 Swiftsure race.*

"TO THE MEMORY OF TRIM, the best and most illustrious of his race, the most affectionate of friends, faithful of servants, and best of creatures … Never will his like be seen again."

Among the nautical books in the Sydney Maritime Museum gift shop, these words and a small black face peering from a poster riveted Larry Trim's attention. "Hey, I want that," he told the sales clerk. "My name is Trim." He also bought a small black book containing Matthew Flinders' (1774–1814) eulogy to his shipmate Trim, "a proper ship's cat of superior intelligence." Born in the southern Indian Ocean in 1799, Trim toured the globe and circumnavigated Australia. Flinders wrote, "He was ever the delight and pleasure of his fellow voyagers." In 1803, a shipwreck deposited Flinders' esteemed cat on the Isle of France, where he perished a year later in the paws of a larger mammal.

have very modern systems today, *Oriole* makes those who sail in her much better understand the elements, the basics of seamanship, and the basics of what a navy is all about. Those things are enduring. They do not change.

"More than that, since *Oriole* has been on the west coast of Canada based in Esquimalt, she has very, very much become part of her community. Many Victorians have had the opportunity to sail in her. She participates in many Swiftsure and Victoria-Maui races. She is a wonderful ambassador, therefore, not only of her navy in Victoria and farther afield, but also of the city itself. The citizens of Victoria have taken *Oriole* and everything she represents to their hearts. They see her as 'their ship.'"

EPILOGUE

*E*ven as CISM's jubilant Finns heaved their victorious skipper off the CFSA finger floats on Friday, June 8, and the departing sailors commended Lieutenant-Commander Larry Trim's workers for their outstanding regatta and race-committee organization, others were finalizing logistics of a different kind—ones that would disrupt future CISM events and mobilize the free world's military to work together toward a common goal.

Three months after CISM's closing ceremonies, the terrorist attacks of September 11, 2001, seared the collective global consciousness. As the Canadian Armed Forces geared up for Operation Apollo, the U.S.-led mission to the Arabian Sea, I thought about my New Zealand shipmates who were sailing from Halifax and Esquimalt into an uncertain future. Larry Trim went to the Arabian Sea to fight the war on terrorism, attached to U.S. aircraft carrier USS *John C. Stennis* as the Canadian liaison officer for the Canadian task group stationed in the area.

Vice-Admiral Ron Buck returned to Victoria from Ottawa in February and March 2002 to participate in the ceremonies when HMCS *Ottawa* and HMCS *Algonquin* deployed to join the international action against terrorism. Minister of National Defence Art Eggleton, Chief of Defence Staff General Ray Henault, British Columbia Lieutenant-Governor Iona Campagnolo, and Vice-Admiral Buck, Chief of Maritime Staff, officiated at the ceremony that sent HMCS *Ottawa* to the war theatre.

In the midst of all this activity, like a time traveller spanning the age of sail and the missile age, the venerable *Oriole* soldiered on with her primary mandate of training the junior officers who will eventually guide Canada's warships into the uncharted horizons of our troubled world. One month after the terrorist attacks, the ketch resumed her community day-sail schedule, with one notable change in the boarding procedures: In keeping with tighter security, her crew now escorted guests to and from the main HMC Dockyard gate.

Operation Apollo made one veteran waterfront observer rethink the navy's community-relations role. Many decades of Swiftsure, Vic-Maui, and Classic Boat Festival participation have woven the *Oriole* and the Naden Band into our maritime cultural mythology. "It's important for the taxpayers to see the real face of the navy, and the value we are getting from the navy," says Classic Boat Festival chairman John West. "We watch the warships heading for the Gulf, but we don't have contact on the civic level. The *Oriole* and the Band are it."

The Odyssey 2002 cruise teamed the *Oriole* with other highly visible navy good-will ambassadors in a joint mission that is central to their individual mandates: benefitting school, community, and registered non-profit groups. From February 5 to

11, the Salty Soaks Dixieland Band from the Naden Band of Maritime Forces Pacific port-hopped up Vancouver Island's east coast, pulling strings by day and performing by night. It was challenging for the musicians to refocus their energies after eight hours of physically taxing tasks on the *Oriole* deck. In addition, many had to stand a watch after their show.

"Our schedule was a real eye-opener for the crew," says Dixieland leader Andy Reljic, Petty Officer, 1st Class. "We as professionals did a lot to represent them and ourselves. I don't think anyone consciously goes out thinking they are going to make a major difference. But I know that we do, though, inspire people."

The Naden Band's presence at ship deployments serves more than a ceremonial purpose. "When HMCS *Ottawa* slipped, a lot of families thanked us for being there," says Reljic. "It was very positive, but also a highly emotional time, because there is always that level of uncertainty."

His words were echoed by Rear-Admiral Jamie Fraser, commander, Maritime Forces Pacific, speaking at the launch for Bandfest 2002, Victoria's International Military Music Festival in June. "It is well known that in peacetime, military musicians are ambassadors for the Canadian Forces and Canada, at home and away. I suggest to you that since September 11, military bands are an important part of the visual reassurance of Canadians against the uncertainty of the world."

Perhaps his words about military musicians can also define HMCS *Oriole*'s enduring value to national and international civilian, sporting, and military communities.

Can we find consolation and comfort—and hope—in the graceful silhouette of HMCS *Oriole*, which symbolizes the essence of a more stable world? And the generosity of spirit, moral integrity, and spiritual values that the Gooderham fathers instilled in their children and extended to their civic and sporting communities? Like Canada's first family of yachting, her motto could also be *toujours en avant*: Always forward.

GLOSSARY

Abaft the beam: An object bears more than 90 degrees from dead ahead.

Abeam: At right angles to a ship's fore-and-aft line.

Aft: Toward or near the stern.

Ahead: In the direction of the bow.

Aloft: Above the deck (floor).

Apparent wind: Direction the wind appears to be going in relation to the speed of the vessel.

Backstay: A stay that supports the mast.

Ballast: Stabilizing material carried to lower a vessel's centre of gravity.

Batten: A flexible strip of wood or fibreglass that fits into a pocket in the leech, giving an even flow of wind across the sail (usually the mainsail).

Beam: The widest part of a ship measured from side to side.

Bearing: Direction an object lies from an observer; in navigation, the angle between the observer and the north (magnetic in coastal navigation).

Boom: The horizontal spar that the foot of the sail is attached to.

Bow: The extreme forward section of a ship.

Bowsprit: A spar running out from the bow, to which the forestays are fastened.

Brow: A gangway between two ships, or from ship to jetty.

Centreboard: A board that can be raised and lowered from the bottom of the boat as a keel.

Cleat: A fitting that a line is secured to.

Clew: The lower aft corner of a sail.

Companionway: The passageway down into a boat's cabin.

Corrected time: The amount of time actually elapsed in a race compared to the boat's ideal speed.

Cutter: A yacht with one mast and two or more headsails, the outer set from the end of a bowsprit.

Fix: A boat's position taken simultaneously from two or more bearings.

Gennaker: An asymmetrical spinnaker that is flown without using a pole. Shorter on the leech than the luff (leading edge of a fore-and-aft sail).

Genoa: Large headsail.

GPS (Global Positioning System): A satellite-reflecting electronic device that indicates one's position on the earth's surface.

Gybe: The main boom sweeps from one side of the boat to the other while running before the wind.

Halyard: A line used to haul a sail up the mast.

Heave to: To stop and maintain position.

Heel: The leeward lean of the boat.

Jib: A triangle-shaped sail forward of the mast.

Jumbo: Storm headsail.

Jury-rig: To assemble temporary, makeshift rigging.

Ketch: Yacht with fore-and-aft rig on two masts. The aftermast (mizzen) is stepped forward of the rudder.

Knot: 6,080 feet per hour.

Leech: After edge of a fore-and-aft sail.

Lifeline: A cable "fence" surrounding the deck—a guardrail.

Luff: The front edge of a sail.

Mainsail: Largest sail mounted on mainmast.

Mizzenmast: Aftmost mast on a ketch.

Nautical mile: One sea mile; 6,080 feet/1,853.25 metres, 1/60 of a degree on the equator.

Reach: A point of sail where the wind is somewhere over the beam (on the beam is a beam reach and abaft the beam is a broad reach).

Reef: To shorten sail.

Rhumb Line: A line cutting all meridians at a constant angle, not a right angle.

Rigging: Running rigging moves (sheets and halyards, for example, hoist and shape sails); standing rigging doesn't move (stays and shrouds, for example).

Round up: Turning the bow into the wind.

Sheer: The upward curve in a deck.

Sheet: A line used to control the sail.

Shroud: Rigging that supports the mast against sideways motion.

Sloop: Yacht with one mast, mainsail, and jib.

Schooner: A fore-and-aft-rigged sailing vessel with two or more masts. If two masts, the aft mast is taller than the fore mast.

Spinnaker: An extra-large, symmetrical sail flown when the wind is abaft the beam, as in running before a "following wind." Also called a chute or kite.

Staysail: Headsail that hanks, or loops, onto a stay and is often named for the stay.

Stern: The rear of a boat.

Tack: A yacht's course in relation to the wind.

Trim: To adjust the sails or their position.

True wind: The direction the wind is going.

Whiskers: The webbing underneath the bowsprit.

Yawl: A yacht with two masts, the mizzen aft of the rudder.

PHOTO CREDITS

Cover and p.11: Navy Public Affairs

Chapter-start images of the battlefield fender on *Oriole*'s deck: Shirley Hewett

p. 12: Courtesy Bryan Judd

p. 14: Paddy Thomson, Royal Vancouver Yacht Club (RVYC)

p. 15: Shirley Hewett

p. 16: Paddy Thomson, RVYC; inset: Shirley Hewett

p. 18: Courtesy Lester B. Pearson College of the Pacific

p. 19: Mary Coakley

p. 21: HMCS *Oriole* archives

pp. 25, 26, 29: Shirley Hewett

pp. 34, 35, 37: Gooderham family archives

p. 39, 40: Royal Canadian Yacht Club (RCYC) archives

p. 41: Gooderham family archives

p. 44: RCYC archives

p. 46-47: Line drawings courtesy of Massachusetts Institute of Technology, Hart Nautical Collection

p. 49: DND

p. 50: Top: Courtesy RVYC; bottom left: Paddy Thomson, RVYC; bottom right: Shirley Hewett

p. 51: Top: Courtesy HMCS *Oriole* archives; middle: courtesy Doug Fryer; bottom: Paddy Thomson, RVYC

p. 52: Top: Paddy Thomson, RVYC; bottom: HMCS *Oriole* archives

p. 53: Gooderham family archives

p. 54: Top: DND; bottom: courtesy Al Horner

p. 55: Top and bottom right: Courtesy HMCS *Oriole* archives; bottom left: Shirley Hewett

p. 56: Top: Courtesy Andrew Madding; bottom: DND

p. 58: *Crowsnest* magazine

p. 59: Courtesy Eve Pangman

p. 60: *Crowsnest* magazine

pp. 62-63: Courtesy Gordon Mills

pp. 65, 66, 67, 70, 71: *Crowsnest* magazine

p. 73: HMC Dockyard

p. 74: DND photo courtesy of Glenda Kirk

p. 76: *Crowsnest* magazine

p. 77: CFB Esquimalt Naval and Military Museum

pp. 78-79: Ron Walker collection

p. 81: Courtesy Bryan Judd

p. 82: James McVie, from *Crowsnest* magazine

p. 84, 86: Courtesy Bob MacLean

p. 88: *Crowsnest* magazine

p. 90: Courtesy of Commander Richard Meadows, RCN (retired)

p. 94: Heritage House Collection. Inset: DND

p. 95: Courtesy James Butterfield

p. 96: Courtesy Commander Eric Wallischeck, United States Merchant Marine Academy

pp. 97-98: Courtesy of Heather Hilliard

p. 101: Courtesy Peter Cox

p. 102: CFSA archives

pp. 104-105: Shirley Hewett

p. 106: Top left: Shirley Hewett; top right: courtesy Ken Brown; bottom: Shirley Hewett

REFERENCES

MAGAZINES AND NEWSPAPERS

Canadian Yachting
The Crowsnest
48 Degrees North
The Globe and Mail
The Chronicle-Herald (Halifax)
Maclean's
Pacific Yachting
The Province (Vancouver)
SAIL
Sailing Canada
Times Colonist (Victoria)
The Vancouver Sun
Victoria Times
Victoria Colonist
Wooden Boat

NEWSLETTERS

RCYC newsletter *Kwasind*
The Sentinel
The Lookout
HMCS Venture *Signal*
HMCS Venture *Venturian*

BOOKS

Bluenose I, II, by Silver Donald Cameron
Beyond the Blue Bridge: Stories from Esquimalt, compiled by the Esquimalt Silver Threads Writers' Group

OTHER SOURCES

HMCS *Oriole* archives
HMCS *Oriole* Proceedings, DND archives
CFB Esquimalt Naval and Military Museum archives
Maritime Museum of British Columbia archives
RCYC Archives
Oriole II logbooks
Royal Victoria Yacht Club Swiftsure archives

WEBSITES

ASTA: www.tallships.sailtraining.org
HMCS *Oriole*: www.vicsurf.com/hmcsoriole
Joe Prosser: www.usmma.edu/waterfront/
MarPac: www.marpac.dnd.ca
Massachusetts Institute of Technology: http://web.mit.edu/museum
Naden Band of Maritime Forces Pacific: www.marpac.dnd.ca/band/band1.htm
Naval Reserve: http://www.navreshq.queb.dnd.ca/HQ-QG/organisa/estab_e.htm
PIRATE at the Center for Wooden Boats: R-boat.org
Swiftsure: www.swiftsure.org
Vic-Maui Race: http://www.vicmaui.org
CFB Esquimalt Naval and Military Museum: www.navalandmilitarymuseum.org

INDEX

Shirley Hewett is a twentieth-generation mariner. Her ancestors arrived in the *Mayflower* and relocated to Nova Scotia's South Shore, where they built and sailed schooners in Shelburne, Barrington, and Lunenburg. Shirley launched Canada's first bare boat charter operation, Bosun's Charter Ltd. She interprets the waterfront community in Victoria, British Columbia, where she has "messed around in boats" for most of her life, through stories in *Monday* magazine, the *Times Colonist* "Islander," *SAIL, Pacific Yachting, 48 Degrees North, Beautiful British Columbia, Mariner Life*, and for CFAX-1070 Swiftsure International Yacht Race broadcasts. Her non-fiction titles include two corporate histories, and she co-authored *Swiftsure, the First Fifty Year*s.